Understanding Put and Call Options

Understanding Put and Call Options

HOW TO USE THEM TO REDUCE RISK IN YOUR STOCK MARKET OPERATIONS

by Herbert Filer

Foreword by
OLIVER GINGOLD, editor "Abreast of the Market,"
The Wall Street Journal

CROWN PUBLISHERS, INC. • *NEW YORK*

The Author has had more than 40 years of active experience in Put and Call transactions. However, he is not authorized to render any legal or tax advice, and nothing contained in this book is intended to be any such advice.

All statements concerning Put and Call transactions are the personal opinions of the Author, based upon his knowledge of the usages and practices ordinarily followed in Put and Call transactions; all problems and questions concerning the legal or tax aspects of Put and Call transactions should be referred to the reader's personal counsel.

Contents

FOREWORD

OPTIONS are probably as old as history. The early Phoenician merchants, and later the Romans, sold what we would term "options" on the goods in their incoming argosies. Later, some three centuries ago, options were used in various ways in Holland and became an important factor in many markets.

Mr. Herbert Filer has dedicated his business life to the subject of stock market options, particularly Puts and Calls. The author of this book has been not only one of the largest option dealers in the world, but he has also been recognized as the top authority. He has lectured and written pamphlets on this seemingly abstruse subject for many years. There are so many facets to the use of options that no single lecture or pamphlet can cover the subject—a full-scale book is required. We can all be grateful to Mr. Filer for composing this comprehensive book, which will be useful to tyros and also serve as a noteworthy addition to the desk of anyone interested in securities.

—OLIVER J. GINGOLD

New York, N. Y.
September, 1959.

THE USE OF OPTIONS

It is strange that a business which has been in existence as long as the business of stock options has never been fully explained, except in leaflet form. As far as I can learn after searching through libraries and college reference books, no complete book has ever been written explaining all of the uses and facets of the business. I have written numerous articles about options, including one for and at the request of the *Encyclopedia Britannica,* and the present edition contains that explanation of the uses of options. But in this book I propose to give the history of options and the various uses of the Put option contract, the Call option, and their variations and combinations such as the Spread, Strip, Straddle, and Strap. Now I will say simply that a Put option is an option to sell (or "Put") at a specific price within a specified time limit. A Call option is an option to buy (or "Call for") at a specified price within a specified time. These will be thoroughly explained shortly, as will Spreads and Straddles. I will show by example just how they can be used in market operations—their speculative uses and their protective or insurance features. I will show that the main advantage in the buying of options is the feature of limited loss and unlimited possible profit. I will also show who "makes" options and why, and the advantages accruing to those who write or make these contracts. Any disadvantages will also be pointed out, because there can be disadvantages if certain age-old principles are ignored.

When I read a book on a special subject, I am curious

about how qualified the writer is to handle the subject; I suppose the reader might want to know my qualifications for writing this book, so here goes.

I started in the option business in 1919—that's forty-three years ago—and today mine is the largest stock-option business in the United States, if not the world. My firm, Filer, Schmidt & Co., has dealt in nothing but options—"Options Exclusively"—for all these years. Options are not just a department of the firm. In 1932, when the Securities Act was being drawn up, the original attitude of the lawmakers was, ". . . not knowing the difference between good options and bad options, for the matter of convenience we strike them all out." At that point the entire option business was threatened, and by appointment of the Put and Call Brokers and Dealers Association, Inc., I had the privilege of appearing before a committee of the House of Representatives and the committee of finance of the Senate to defend the usefulness and economic value of our business in the securities market. Subsequently, the Securities and Exchange Commission was formed, and the option business was allowed to function "if not in contravention of rules set down by the SEC." In all these years the SEC has not found it necessary to lay down any rules to govern the business of Put and Call options.

Almost all of the option business in this country is done by some twenty-five members of the Put and Call Brokers and Dealers Association, Inc. This association forms rules for the conduct of the business, polices the affairs of its members, arbitrates any differences between its members or between its members and the public, and reports each week to the Securities and Exchange Commission a list of option trades made by the members of the association. While the options traded through our members run into millions of shares annually, there is rarely a matter which comes before our Board of Arbitration, and seldom is an error made in making a trade.

During my forty-three years in the business, I have lectured to trainees of stock-exchange houses as well as to representatives of stock-exchange firms from coast to coast, also to groups of professors of finance from various colleges and universities who visit New York each spring. I have lectured on the subject of stock options for a number of colleges and universities, and it has been my pleasure to have lectured for a number of years to the class in finance of the University of Vermont, which each year visits Wall Street for a six-week course of instruction in various phases of finance. I have also studied the option business in London, Paris, Amsterdam, and Switzerland, after which we patterned the option business as we operate it today in this country. Option business was done in Europe long before any of our exchanges was organized.

Of course, during the years of World War II, there was no trading on the European exchanges, for they were then closed. However, since the end of the war there has been trading on such exchanges where currency is free (for instance, in Switzerland), and today we do considerable option business between New York and Switzerland. It might be of interest to the reader to know that on the London Exchange, where option trading had been discontinued since the war even though securities, as such, were traded, the members voted overwhelmingly for options, and actual trading was resumed in October, 1958. London options, however, are different from American contracts in many respects, the two important differences being that options can be traded only between members—not the public—and London options cannot be "done," as they term it, for periods over seven account periods (approximately ninety days). In the United States we do a large part of our option business in six-month options and, occasionally, trade in contracts for one year. And our contracts can be bought or sold by members of an exchange or the public.

Options were used in Holland about three hundred years ago in the boom of tulip bulbs. A grower engaging to deliver a shipment of tulip bulbs and concerned over the safe arrival of his shipment, would, for a small sum, acquire an option from another grower on a like amount of bulbs at the current price. If for some reason the boat carrying his cargo did not arrive at its destination and the shipment of tulip bulbs was lost, through his option he could reacquire the tulips of the other grower and thereby be able to make good on his contract to deliver without having to pay the possibly much higher price prevailing at the time of delivery.

Although his insurance could cover the value of the original shipment, it could not protect him against a much higher replacement cost. His option gave him the needed insurance against a price increase or costly breach of contract.

Options are used daily in real estate transactions, and such use is explained here in an attempt to draw a parallel, as near as possible, between options on stocks and options on real estate.

A builder wants to buy a large plot of ground in order to build an office building or an apartment house. On this plot of ground there are a number of small buildings which he plans to demolish so that he can erect his building—but *only* if he can acquire the entire plot of ground. To buy some of the buildings only to find out that he cannot purchase all, would prevent the erection of the complete project and would be costly and risky. So for a relatively small sum the builder tries to acquire an option on each building, and having acquired such options he can buy all of the properties through these options and commence the building project. If, however, the company is unable to obtain options on all of the property, it can abandon its plans and its loss would be limited to the cost of the options acquired.

As another illustration, let us suppose that Mr. Jones wants to sell a piece of property for $100,000, and Mr. Smith believes that he can sell it to Mr. White for $125,000. Mr. Smith wouldn't want to buy the property and then find that he was unable to sell to Mr. White. So for a relatively small sum he buys an option from Mr. Jones, good for 90 days, to buy the property for $100,000. If, within the 90 days Mr. Smith is successful in making the sale to Mr. White for $125,000, he *then* exercises his option and buys the property from Mr. Jones according to the terms of his option contract, and sells it to Mr. White. Mr. Smith has made $25,000, less the cost of his option. If, however, he had been unable to sell the property to Mr. White, Mr. Smith would have allowed his option to lapse and his loss would have been limited to the cost of the option contract.

Options are used extensively in many businesses today. A ball club has an option on a player, a movie studio on an actor or actress, and you can even choose your own option as to how you wish to have your life insurance paid to your heirs.

Webster's Dictionary gives these definitions of "option":

(1) The exercise of the power of choice.
(2) Power of choosing: the right of choice, an alternative.
(3) A stipulated privilege of buying or selling a stated property, security or commodity at a given price within a specified time.
(4) The right of an insured person to choose the form in which payments due to him on a policy shall be made or applied.

In the case of Put and Call stock options, the choice or "option" belongs to the holder of the option contract; he can exercise his contract or not, according to his choice, and he will exercise the option *at or before* its expiration *only* if it is to his advantage to do so. The seller of the option has *no* choice; once he has sold the contract, he must accept stock or deliver stock according to the terms of the option and *only at the option of the one who holds the contract.*

Options are sometimes confused with "hedging" or "arbitraging"—*they are neither;* for again to use Webster's definitions:

Arbitrage—Purchasing in one market for immediate sale
in another at a higher price.

Hedge—To counterbalance a sale or purchase of one security by making a purchase or sale of another.

Neither of the above-described operations can be compared to option-trading. Neither the arbitrageur nor the
hedger has any option; he has made two complete trades.
The holder of a Put or Call option exercises his option
contract *only* if it is to his advantage to do so. He has one
side of his trade in his option contract and the other side
—the buying against a Put or the selling against a Call—is
done only if it is profitable to the one who holds the
option contract.

Options can be used as a speculative medium with
small, or relatively small, risk and with *unlimited* possible
profit. The leverage in connection with option-trading is
exceedingly attractive. In any venture, the relation of the
possible profit to the possible loss is something that cannot be overlooked. The uses to which options can be put
are numerous, and because the general public and even
the brokerage fraternity are not well versed in the various
uses of options, this book will explain in considerable
detail many of the general uses and even the intricacies of
option-dealing.

Colleges and universities have begun to realize that this
subject, which is part of Wall Street procedure, could well
be included in a course on finance. I feel that the information gained through such education will stand the students
in good stead when they enter the business world, particularly the field of finance.

15

It is my contention that options are protective contracts—they protect either before or after a stock commitment. A man can buy an option to protect a purchase or sale already made or about to be made. He can acquire a Put contract to protect stock which he holds. He can buy a Put to protect him against unlimited loss when he buys a stock. He can buy a Put to protect a profit which he already has and doesn't want to lose. Or he can acquire a Put or a Call to protect him against a commitment which he expects to make at a later date and on which, when he makes such commitment, he does not want to take an unlimited risk. So an option is a protective device no matter when it is used.

It is not my contention that everyone must trade in options, but I do say that anyone who has an interest in securities should have a knowledge of Put and Call options because at some time or other options can play a part in one's security-trading, whether to protect a profit or possibly to recapture stock after taking a profit.

From figures recently gathered, there are about 12,000,000 stockholders in the United States. I will venture to say that of these 12,000,000 stockholders, not even 12,000 have more than a smattering of knowledge of Put and Call options, and not more than 1,200 out of the 12,000,000 could explain very much of the technical workings of the option contract. Take my word for it—to understand the workings of options is not very difficult and any effort to unravel this supposed mystery will be rewarding to the stockbroker and also to his customer.

The use of options spread into the securities business as a protective and also a speculative device. In the late nineteenth century, options in this country acquired the names of "Puts" and "Calls," and they have been dealt in in increasing numbers ever since, for those who deal in securities recognize both their protective and their speculative value.

Put-Call options can be used profitably in either a rising or a falling market, and the increasing interest in them is a result of the knowledge gained by the public of the various uses to which options can be put.

Of course a man wouldn't think of owning a home without insuring it against fire; nor would he think of not insuring his wife's jewelry and furs against loss or theft; he carries life insurance to protect his family when he dies. Yet it is strange that relatively few people understand that through Put and Call options they can protect themselves against unlimited loss in stock-holdings, or can preserve substantial "paper" profits without selling. Many of the large losses, either of invested capital or "paper" profits, sustained by traders in the bad breaks in the market that come every now and then, could have been avoided through the protection that is available through options. It has been my experience that small stock-losses do not break a man, but it is the large loss taken by the stubborn trader in a market like that of 1929, 1937, 1946, or 1957 that can wipe out a trader or leave him with little chance to recoup his losses.

Now seems to be the time when options are needed in the field of finance more than ever before because they act as a protection against excessive losses and as a safeguard for profits. It should be made known to every investor and speculator that there is a way to guard against exces-

17

sive losses by limiting such losses to a specified and relatively small amount.

Option-Dealers

Practically all the orders for the purchase and sale of Put and Call options come to New York, where they are executed by members of the Put and Call Brokers and Dealers Association, Inc. As previously explained, this association consists of approximately twenty-five members who deal exclusively in Put and Call options, and all of the options in which these members deal are guaranteed by member firms of the New York Stock Exchange. The option contracts in which the members deal are transferable contracts, and on the back of each contract is the name of the stock-exchange firm where the individual or company that sold the contract has his account. This endorsement of a member firm of the New York Stock Exchange guarantees that the terms of the contract will be met. The contract is made out in bearer form and can be resold by one person to another.

The option-dealer is a middleman; he arranges for the purchase of and/or sale of options between a possible buyer and a seller. It is his business to try to sell options which are offered and, conversely, to try to buy options which his clients want to obtain. The option-dealer works with, not against, his client and rarely takes the position of maker of the option. His profit is made between what he pays for an option and what he sells it for.

Option Contracts

Option contracts are traded in units of 100 shares, *not*

in odd lots, and they are made for periods of 30 days, 60 days, 90 days, 6 months "plus," and, occasionally, for one year. Puts and Calls are usually done "at the market." That is, the price at which the stock is selling when the trade is made. A Put or a Call on a stock selling at 50 would be made at 50 in the usual way of business. However, it is possible to buy or sell an option "away from the market," that is a Call at 52 when the stock is selling at 50 or any differential by agreement. The most popular contracts are those that run for 90 days or 6 months. A contract can be exercised at any time before expiration at the option of the holder. It is not necessary to wait until expiration to act on or exercise one's option. If a man owns a Call option at 50 which expires on December 10, and by November 20 the stock has risen to 60—at which point he would be satisfied with such a profit—he may exercise his option at that time. He need not wait until the expiration of the contract.

Option Money

The option money or premium is the amount paid for the contract. The amount paid for the option is not applied to adjust the price at which stock is bought or sold upon the exercise of the option. If you have a Call on stock at 70 and you exercise the option, you pay $70 a share for the stock less any dividends that accrue to the contract. If you have a Put at 70 and you exercise the Put, you receive $70 a share for the stock less any dividends that are due on the option contract.

For Value Received, the BEARER may DELIVER

stock of the ____ - - XYZ CORPORATION

at ____ - - SEVENTY - -

ANY TIME WITHIN ____ - - NINETY - -

THIS STOCK OPTION CONTRACT MUST BE ?
EXPIRATION OF THE EXACT TIME LIMIT. IT CANN

DURING THE LIFE OF THIS OPTION:
1. (a) — the contract price hereof shall be redu
(b) — where the Option is entitled to rights and/or wa
opening sale thereof on the day the stock sells ex-rights .
2. (a) — in the event of stock splits, reverse spli
become an Option for the equivalent in new securities
(b) — stock dividends or the equivalent due-bills shall be
the total contract price shall not be reduced.
Upon presentation to the endorser of this Option
agrees to accept notice of the Bearer's exercise by stan
shall be controlling with respect to delivery of the stock

EXPIRES ____ AUGUST 20th 19 59
3:15 P. M.

W N⁰ 168

NEGOTIATED BY

Filer, Schmidt & Co.
ESTABLISHED 1919

Member Put and Call Brokers and Dealers Association, Inc.

PUT AND CALL OPTIONS

GUARANTEED BY MEMBERS N. Y. STOCK EXCHANGE

120 BROADWAY, N. Y. C. 5   BARCLAY 7-6100

A PUT OPTION CONTRACT

A Put option is a transferable-bearer contract paid for by the
buyer upon delivery of the contract, giving him the right, at
his option, to deliver to the maker or seller of the contract
a certain number of shares of stock at a fixed price *on or before
a stipulated date.*

20

In the above contract the holder may deliver to the endorser
of the contract 100 shares of XYZ common stock at 70 any time
before the expiration date (August 20) *at his option.*

The exercise of a contract is not automatic. The contract
must be presented to the cashier of the endorsing firm *before
expiration.*

The above contract has been approved by the Put and Call
Brokers and Dealers Association, Inc. and is used by members
of that association.

This is the reverse side of a Put contract and will be signed by a member firm of the New York Stock Exchange, guaranteeing to the holder of the Put contract that the stock will be accepted if the holder of the Put wishes to exercise his option.

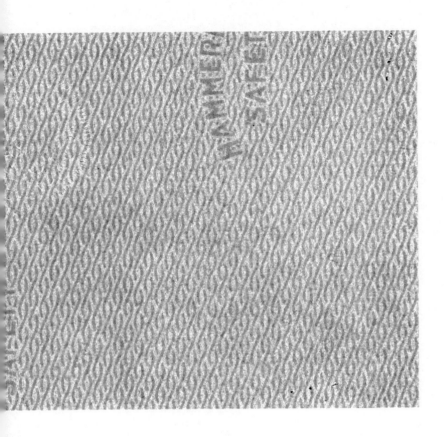

23

For Value Received, the BEARER may CALL o
stock of the - - XYZ CORPORATION -
at - - SEVENTY - -
ANY TIME WITHIN - - NINETY -
THIS STOCK OPTION CONTRACT MUST BE
EXPIRATION OF THE EXACT TIME LIMIT. IT CANN

DURING THE LIFE OF THIS OPTION:
1. (a) — the contract price hereof shall be redu
(b) — where the Option is entitled to rights and/or wa
opening sale thereof on the day the stock sells ex-rights
2. (a) — in the event of stock splits, reverse spl
become an Option for the equivalent in new securities
(b) — stock dividends or the equivalent due-bills shall b
the total contract price shall not be reduced.
Upon presentation to the endorser of this Option
agrees to accept notice of the Bearer's exercise by sta
shall be controlling with respect to delivery of the stock

EXPIRES___AUGUST 20th___19_59
3:15 P.M.

P N⁰ 554

NEGOTIATED BY

Filer, Schmidt & Co.

ESTABLISHED 1919

Member Put and Call Brokers and Dealers Association, Inc.

PUT AND CALL OPTIONS

GUARANTEED BY MEMBERS N. Y. STOCK EXCHANGE

120 BROADWAY, N. Y. C. 5 BARCLAY 7-6100

CALL OPTION CONTRACT

A Call option is a transferable bearer contract paid for by the buyer upon delivery of the contract, giving him the right, at his option, to buy or "Call" from the maker or seller of such

New York, N. Y._____ MAY 22nd,____19 59

rser for ONE HUNDRED (100) shares of the_____COMMON

_____Dollars ($ 70.00_____) per share

_____days from date.

, AS SPECIFIED BELOW, TO THE ENDORSING FIRM BEFORE THE
RCISED BY TELEPHONE.

e value of any cash dividend on the day the stock goes ex-dividend;
contract price shall be reduced by the value of same as fixed by the
rants.
r similar action by the above-mentioned corporation, this Option shall
listed for trading and the total contract price shall not be reduced;
to the stock covered hereby, when and if this Option is exercised, and

to a comparison ticket in the manner and time specified, the endorser
comparison, and this acknowledgment shall constitute a contract and
ment in accordance with New York Stock Exchange usage.

The undersigned acts as intermediary only,
without obligation other than to obtain a
New York Stock Exchange firm as Endorser.

MEMBER

& CALL

& DEALERS
TION, INC.

Filer Schmidt & Co

CALL OPTION

contract a certain number of shares of stock at a fixed price,
on or before a stipulated date.

In the above contract the holder may call for or buy from the
endorser of the contract 100 shares of XYZ common stock at 70
any time before the expiration date (August 20) at his option.

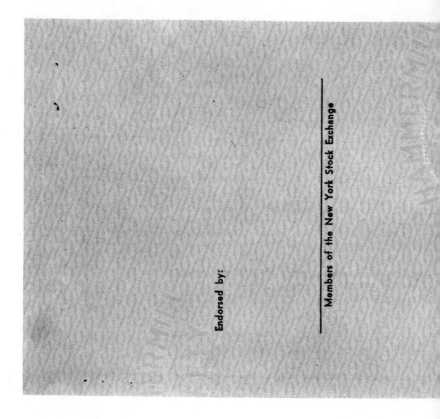

Endorsed by:

Members of the New York Stock Exchange

This is the reverse side of a Call contract whereon is put the endorsement or guarantee of a stock-exchange house guaranteeing to the holder of the Call that the stock specified in the contract will be delivered to him, at his option, upon presentation of the Call contract.

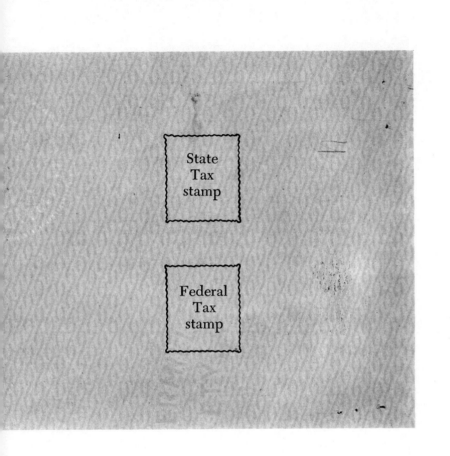

State
Tax
stamp

Federal
Tax
stamp

THIS IS A QUOTATION SHEET DATED MAY 25, 1959

This is what we call a *nominal* quotation sheet from May 25, 1959, which is sent along with explanatory literature to those who inquire about our business. It is merely an approximate price at which options are quoted on a representative list of stocks on which options are written. However, options are written on a much longer list of stocks than those indicated; in fact, options can be arranged on most common stocks listed on the New York Stock Exchange, some stocks listed on the American Stock Exchange, and at times on stocks traded in the over-the-counter market. Anyone interested in the buying or selling of an option can obtain quotations through his stock-exchange broker or directly from an option dealer.

These quotes are nominal. Latest quotations should be obtained from your Stock Exchange broker, or directly from us.

QUOTATIONS FURNISHED BY

Filer, Schmidt & Co.

ESTABLISHED 1919

Members Put & Call Brokers & Dealers Ass'n, Inc.

THE PUT & CALL MARKET

120 BROADWAY, NEW YORK 5, N. Y.   BArclay 7-6100

All contracts are endorsed by Members Firms of the New York Stock Exchange
The following quotations are on the issues that are most active in the Option Market
Other Quotations May Be Had On Request

	Price for 90 day Put at Market	Price for 90 day Call at Market	Price for 6 mos. Put at Market	Price for 6 mos. Call at Market
American Cyanamid	$425.00	$475.00	$550.00	$675.00
Am. Smelt. & Ref.	400.00	450.00	525.00	650.00
Anaconda	450.00	525.00	675.00	750.00
Atchison, T. & S. F.	225.00	275.00	300.00	350.00
Amer. Tel. & Tel. WI	475.00	550.00	700.00	850.00
Bethlehem Steel	350.00	425.00	475.00	550.00
Balt. & Ohio	300.00	350.00	450.00	525.00
Case, J. I., Co.	225.00	275.00	325.00	400.00
Celanese Corp.	275.00	325.00	375.00	450.00
Chrysler Corp.	450.00	550.00	650.00	800.00
Crucible Steel	275.00	325.00	375.00	425.00
Deere	475.00	550.00	600.00	725.00
Douglas Aircraft	425.00	475.00	650.00	700.00
General Electric	500.00	600.00	750.00	850.00
Goodrich, B. F., Co.	700.00	750.00	850.00	1000.00
Goodyear T. & R. Co.	750.00	800.00	1000.00	1300.00
Hertz	375.00	450.00	550.00	625.00
Illinois Central	350.00	400.00	475.00	550.00
Inter'l Nickel	500.00	525.00	725.00	825.00
Inter'l Paper	700.00	800.00	1000.00	1200.00
Inter'l Tel. & Tel.	350.00	400.00	475.00	575.00
Jones & Laughlin	475.00	525.00	625.00	725.00
Kennecott Copper	650.00	700.00	825.00	975.00
Martin	475.00	525.00	700.00	825.00
Montgomery Ward	300.00	350.00	425.00	475.00
N. Y. Central	250.00	300.00	350.00	425.00
Northern Pacific	375.00	425.00	500.00	575.00
Pennsylvania R.R.	225.00	250.00	275.00	325.00
Richfield Oil	700.00	775.00	950.00	1050.00
Republic Steel	450.00	500.00	650.00	700.00
Schenley Ind.	300.00	350.00	400.00	500.00
Southern Pacific	500.00	525.00	650.00	725.00
Southern Railway	350.00	400.00	525.00	600.00
S. O. of Calif.	350.00	400.00	525.00	600.00
S. O. Co. of N. J.	375.00	425.00	550.00	625.00
United Aircraft	450.00	500.00	625.00	700.00
U. S. Rubber	450.00	525.00	650.00	725.00
U. S. Steel	500.00	550.00	750.00	825.00
Western Union	300.00	350.00	475.00	550.00
Westinghouse Elec.	500.00	650.00	800.00	900.00
Youngstown S. & T.	700.00	800.00	1000.00	1100.00

**Orders for these or other contracts can be placed directly with us
or through your Stock Exchange Broker by SPECIFYING
"BUY FROM FILER, SCHMIDT & CO."**

State and Federal tax must be added to the cost of call options.

NO TAX ON PUT OPTIONS.   Quotations Subject To Change Without Notice.

The options described above are facsimiles of the contracts used by members of the Put and Call Brokers and Dealers Association, Inc., of New York. They are bearer transferable contracts endorsed or guaranteed by member firms of the New York Stock Exchange and can be sold or transferred at will, like checks. The law requires that New York state and federal tax stamps be affixed to Call options but not to Put options; stamps so affixed are the same as if the stock in question had been sold in the market. The tax is based on the selling price of the stock, but is never more than $12.00 for the combined federal and state tax per each 100-share Call. The New York state tax is as follows:

On stocks—

under $5, the tax is $1, to be affixed to each 100-share Call contract;

$5 and over but under $10, the tax is $2, to be affixed to each 100-share Call contract;

$10 and over but under $20, the tax is $3, to be affixed to each 100-share Call contract;

on $20 and over, the tax is $4, to be affixed to each 100-share Call contract.

The federal tax is based on the *dollar value* of the stock specified as follows in the Call contract for each 100-share Call:

FEDERAL TAX
$.04 per $100 value
$.04 any fraction above ½

30

as an example:

$$(.04/100.00 \text{ of } \$4000.00)$$

$40.00 STOCK	=	$1.60
40½ "	=	1.60
40⅝ "	=	1.64
50½ "	=	2.00
50⅝ "	=	2.04

The maximum federal tax is $8.

The combined *maximum* federal and state tax is $12 per 100-share Call.

Holidays

Options are never made to expire on a *known* holiday. The contract will be made to expire on the next business day after the holiday.

The Offering of Special Options

Besides arranging for the purchase and sale of new options on order, some option-dealers carry an inventory of option contracts which they offer for resale through newspaper advertisements, as on page 32 or by quotation sheets sent through the mail. The offerings may be limited in quantity and are offered "subject to prior sale or price change." Originally, these contracts are bought by an option-dealer in the expectation and hope that he can resell them. If the dealer holds a Call contract and the market favors him, he might very well be able to dispose of the contract at a profit. If the market declines, the option may prove to be a complete loss to the dealer, but this is a business risk that he takes.

31

THE ADVERTISING OR OFFERING OF SPECIAL OPTIONS

The above are advertisements offering special options. The one on the left is from *The New York Times* and the one on the right from the *Wall Street Journal*, both of the June 2, 1959, issues.

The contracts shown in the above advertisements are *offerings,* not bids. Here is the explanation of exactly what the ad means: the first item under "Put Options" means that on receipt of $700, the option-dealer will deliver a Put contract giving to the buyer of the Put (the purchaser or anyone to whom he transfers the Put) the right to *deliver or sell* to endorser or guarantor of the option 100 shares of U. S. Steel at 95½ any time before December 8. At the time of the advertisement, the stock was selling at 94¾, so the Put option was ¾ of a point *above* the market price. At the same time, a newly made 6-month Put option *at the market price* of 94¾ would have cost about $750, so by comparison, the Put at 95½ for $700 was more attractive, since the obtainable price was $75 higher and the cost of the option $50 less. Comparison should be made between regular market options and special options that are advertised, and option-dealers, when asked to quote a price for an option, usually offer special options if they are available.

The converse of the Put option on U. S. Steel at 95½ which was offered when STEEL was selling at 94¾ is the Call offered in *The Times* ad on Jones & Laughlin at 71⅝, running until August 21 for $650.

At the time this Call was offered, the stock was selling at 75, or 3⅜ points *above* the Call price, and the Call had 82 days to run. In other words, the Call already showed a gross profit of 3⅜ points. Compare such an offering if you will with a newly made 90-day Call contract at the *then current market price* of 75 which was offered for $525. To make a profit on the newly made option, the stock would have to advance above 80¼ (not counting stock-exchange commissions). To make a profit on the special Call, the stock would have to advance to 78⅛. That is, 71⅝—the Call price plus the $650 premium paid for the option.

Notice that special options are usually offered at a price different from the market price of the stock. Newly made contracts are usually made at the market price of the stock at the time the contract is arranged.

Straddle Option

A "Straddle" is a combination of a Put and a Call option sold for a single price. The premium is paid by the buyer at the time the contract is made. The Straddle gives the holder the right, at his option, to sell the maker of the contract the stated number of shares of the specified stock at the stated price before the specified date *and also* the right to receive and buy from the maker the stated number of shares of the specified stock at the same price before the same date.

> EXAMPLE: A Put contract at 60 and a Call contract at 60. The exercise of one contract before expiration does *not* void the remaining option.

A "Spread" is similar to a Straddle—a combination of a Put and a Call contract—except that where a Straddle is a combination of a Put and a Call at the same price, the Spread is a Put at a price below the current stock-market price, and the Call is a price above the current stock-market price.

EXAMPLE: Stock selling at 60 in the market. A Spread is a Put possibly at 58 and a Call possibly at 62. A Spread can be made at various distances from the market price, and the dollar cost price of the Spread contract varies with the Spread of the option prices.

The Spread is less expensive than a Straddle on the same stock for the same length of time by approximately half the difference of the spread between the Put and Call. For example, if a Straddle at 60 were to cost $600, a Spread of two points up and two points down would cost $400. The difference of $200 would represent half of the spread between 58 and 62.

Straddle at 60 — Cost $600
Spread 58–62 — Cost $400

Options are dealt with in units of 100 shares—never in odd lots. Nevertheless, orders for 500- or 1,000-share options are common and orders for 10,000-share options occasionally come into the market. However, to buy options on such a quantity of shares is a job which the option-dealer must handle with care. To go to a seller of options and let him know that you have an order of that size would immediately arouse his suspicions and he would be reluctant to sell any options. So, in handling such an order, the option-dealer must try to fill his order 500 or 1,000 shares at a time, without disclosing the size of the full order. The same technique would probably be used on the floor of the stock exchange by a broker who had a large quantity of a stock to buy or sell. To disclose the size of his order would enable other brokers to "take the market away from him," and he would then be able to complete his order only by bidding the stock up in the case of a "buy" order or marking it down considerably in the case of a "sell" order.

Most option business is done in stocks listed on the New York Stock Exchange, some in stocks listed on the American Stock Exchange, and a small part in securities traded in the "over-the-counter" market. While options cannot always be negotiated on every stock on the exchange, the number of stocks on which options are written includes most of the leading stocks and also enough additional issues to satisfy a large demand.

All option contracts expire at 3:15 P.M. (New York time) on the date stated in the contract, and they cannot be exercised by telephone but must be presented to the cashier of the stock-exchange firm that endorses the contract before the expiration time of 3:15 P.M. (New York time). A number of stock-exchange firms who have bought contracts for their customers, to avoid loss, insist on having instructions for the exercise of options well in advance of expiration time on the day that the option expires. In order to eliminate the chance of loss in late presentation of an option and to avoid delay when a contract is to be exercised, *contracts should never be kept outside of New York City* but should remain with your stockbroker or your option-dealer for safekeeping. The maker of an option contract will not accept it if it is presented after it expires. When he sells the option, he agrees to live up to the terms of the contract but not beyond them. If the maker of a contract agreed to accept one presented two minutes after it had expired, he might be asked to accept one twenty minutes or thirty minutes after it had expired, or even on the next day. He is not willing to go beyond the terms or time of his contracted agreement. Thus, holders of contracts that are to be exercised should take extra care to see that ample notice is given to exercise options before expiration time. The holder of a contract should acquaint himself with the rules of his stock-exchange house and the latest time he may give instructions to exercise an option.

To exercise an option, the stock-exchange firm that holds the contract for its customer presents the actual Put or Call contract to the stock-exchange firm that endorsed it, together with a comparison ticket. A comparison ticket is *written* notice to the endorsing house that "We have sold you 100 shares of X at 70 according to the Put contract presented herewith," or, in the case of a Call, "We are buying 100 shares of X at 70, according to the Call contract presented herewith." Delivery of and payment for the actual stock is usually made four days after the trade. In exercising such an option contract, the stock-exchange broker will charge the client a commission for exercising the contract just as if he had sold stock for him on the exchange, in the case of a Put, or had bought stock, in the case of a Call. If the customer supplies his own stock for the Put or retains the stock that he Called, there is no other commission. But if he buys the stock that he Put or sells the stock that he Called, he will pay regular commissions in those transactions, also. To give the uninitiated an idea of the amount of stock-exchange commissions charged by your stockbroker for buying or selling stock either in the market or through the exercise of an option, the following established rate will guide:

For buying or selling 100 shares of a stock at $50 per share, the commission is $44; for buying or selling 100 shares of a stock at $75 per share, the commission is $46.50; for buying or selling 100 shares of a stock at $100, the commission is $49.

In the closing or exercising of an option contract, by buying or selling stock in the market and exercising the option *on the same day*, the customer will be required to deposit with his stockbroker 25 per cent margin (instead of 70° per cent) or $1,000—whichever is higher—because such a trade is a complete and virtually riskless transaction.

Some individuals who are far from an office of a stock-exchange firm or who have no account with one often do business directly with an option-dealer. The option-dealer will hold options for the account of a customer and will exercise the options upon instructions from the customer.

In lieu of closing a contract for a client, the Put and Call Dealer may buy the contract from the client. The price which he will pay will be computed after the Dealer has exercised the contract for his own account and has sold the corresponding stock in the market (in the case of a Call), or has bought the stock in the market (in the case of a Put); the price will be equal to the net proceeds of the Dealer's transactions less two regular stock exchange commisions and any applicable tax. No margin has been required because the customer *will have sold the contract itself* to the Put and Call Dealer.

The customer who expects to buy options directly from

° Federal Reserve fixes margin requirements which are changeable.

an option-dealer should make a deposit with his option-dealer to open an account and thereby avoid any delay in the execution of orders when he desires to buy an option. Any options bought by the client will be debited against his account, and any profit arising from the sale of a contract by a client to an option-dealer will be credited to the client's account. Most dealers ask their clients to send their orders by wire, collect, because if a client gets an idea that a stock is going to move and wants to buy an option, the delay in sending an order through the mail could make him miss the move.

While option-dealers carry accounts for clients who want to *purchase* options, the making or selling of original Put and Call contracts must be arranged with a stock-exchange firm so that the contracts sold will carry that firm's endorsement. The option-dealer will be glad to help make such arrangements for those who do not already have an account with a stock-exchange firm but the option-dealer does not carry customers' securities and members of our association are not members of the New York Stock Exchange and cannot endorse options.

In the purchase of options, timing is most important. Many times, the customer has good information but buys 90-day options or 6-month options, only to have the stock move just after his option expires. For that reason it might be well to consider the purchase of option contracts on the stagger system so that the expiration dates occur a week or so apart. Buy some of your options this week, some next week, etc., as far as you want to go, so that if the first set of options is bought too early, it is possible that those bought subsequently can prove profitable. It is also good policy to buy an option of longer duration than you think you need. If you think that a move may take place in 60 days, it is smart to buy an option for 90 days. The cost of the longer option will ordinarily be very little more.

For many years prior to 1935, options were dealt in for periods of 2 days, 7 days, 15 days, and 30 days—rarely longer. The short-term contract is now quite obsolete— most of our current business is in contracts for 60 days, 90 days, and 6 months. The 6-month option is usually made for 6 months and 10 days to take advantage of the long-term gains provision of the tax law.

The option business is a little different from the stock-exchange business. In the latter, if you want to buy 100 shares of U.S. Steel, you place your order with a broker who, through his man on the floor of the exchange, can buy or sell the stock in a matter of minutes. A ready market will be quoted, e.g., 69½ bid offered at 70. That means that there is a ready market where you can sell stock at 69½ or buy stock at 70. In the over-the-counter market, if you want to buy or sell an unlisted stock such as an insurance or a bank stock, a dealer in those issues will quote you a firm market and will trade immediately. Not so in the option business—here almost all quotes are nominal and subject to being filled, and every trade must be consummated individually and by phone. It may be that when an order is placed to buy or sell an option, as many as fifty phone calls will have to be made by the option-dealer before a trade is completed. He may have to make phone calls to Detroit or Chicago or anywhere in the country. Only through an option-dealer's knowledge of the business can he quote with any accuracy the market on any issue for an option, and only through this knowledge and his contacts can he fill his orders for options with the least delay. Contracts are sometimes offered "firm" for a few minutes and, occasionally, a contract will be offered overnight. The option-dealer usually keeps a file system listing clients who have signified that they have an interest in selling options on various issues, and it is this list of possible sellers of options that the dealer contacts when he has orders to buy either Puts or Calls.

Uses of the Put Option Contract

In all of the following examples, for the sake of better understanding, I will try as much as possible to use one figure for the price of the stock and one figure for the cost of the option. Understand, please, that these prices change in actual practice. The cost of an option on a stock selling at 50 would be less than one selling at 80 and, likewise, the cost of an option for 90 days would be less than one for 6 months on the same stock. The price of an option usually depends on the price of the stock, the duration of the option, the volatility of the stock, and supply and demand for the options in question.

Buying a Put Option for Speculation

A man who thought that a stock selling in the market at 50 would decline to possibly 30 could buy a Put option. In buying an option, he should have some idea to what extent the stock might move. In inquiring what a Put option would cost, he might receive a nominal quote of, say, $350 for a Put at the market for 90 days. Most options are negotiated "at the market," which means at "the current market," when the option can be obtained by the option-dealer. Suppose that the stock is selling at 50 and the quoted price of $350 is satisfactory to you. You enter your order: "Buy a 90-day Put on 100 XYZ [the name of the stock] for $350." If you are trading through your stock-exchange broker, he will give your order to an option-dealer who will contact one of his clients who sells options on that stock and will attempt to buy the option for you. When, after this contact or several others, he has obtained the Put option for you, he reports to the stock-exchange broker who gave him the order, and he in turn reports to the customer: "Bought Put 100 XYZ at 50 expires December 30 for $350." Let us say that the man who bought the Put option, expecting a decline in the stock, was wrong, and that the stock, instead of going to 30 (as he expected), advanced to 70 and was selling there when his option expired. He would have lost the $350 that he paid for his Put option. Bear in mind that the limit of the man's loss was the cost of his Put option, or $350, no matter how high the stock rose and no matter how wrong he was, and that he would draw on the equity in his account to that extent only. Suppose, on the other hand, he had sold the stock short in the market. His loss would have been 20 points and still no knowledge as to the possible extent of loss until he covered the short sale. But in the purchase of the Put option his account would read:

Bought Put on XYZ at 50 for 90 days: Loss $350

Remember, too, that no trade has been made in the stock, so no stock-exchange commission has been paid. A regular stock-exchange commission is charged by your broker only if a transfer of stock is made in connection with the option.

On the other hand, suppose the man's judgment was correct and the stock declined to 30. If he had instructed his stockbroker to buy 100 shares at 30 and exercise his Put option, his account would look like this:

Sold 100 shares at 50 (through exercise of Put)	$5,000
Total Receipts	$5,000
Bought 100 shares in market at 30	3,000
Bought Put at 50	
Cost	350
Total Cost	3,350
Profit on trade	$1,650

The profit then would be almost 500 per cent of the cost of the Put contract. The profit is the difference between the cost of the stock plus the cost of the Put option and the proceeds of the Put that was exercised.

In all of these examples showing the use of options, the commission cost has been ignored. But at no time could the loss have been more than the cost of the option—$350—and any stock-exchange commissions would have been paid out of profit or out of possible recovery of part of the premium which was paid.

Trading in Odd Lots Against a Put Option

In the aforementioned example of trading against an option, the trading was done by buying 100 shares of stock at 30 and selling the stock at 50 through the exercise of a Put option.

Another way of operating against such a Put option is to buy stock in odd lots of, say, 25 shares each on a scale-down as follows: the holder of a Put at 50 might buy 25 shares at 36, 25 shares at 34, 25 shares at 32, and 25 shares at 30. Of course, each purchase in the market must be margined according to stock-exchange regulations, but the man who has no definite opinion as to where the stock should be bought against his option "scales" his buying orders until he has bought 100 shares, and then he may, if he cares to, deliver these shares against his Put option contract.

His account would then read:

Bought 25 shares at 36 cost	$ 900.00
Bought 25 shares at 34 cost	850.00
Bought 25 shares at 32 cost	800.00
Bought 25 shares at 30 cost	750.00
	$3,300.00
Cost of Put	350.00
	$3,650.00
Sold 100 at 50 through exercise of Put	$5,000.00
Profit	$1,350.00

If, however, the contract has some time to run, he may want to hold the stock which he bought, looking for a rally and a chance to sell his stock in the market and thereby leave himself open to repeat the operation, if possible.

Trading Several Times Against an Option

Suppose that instead of expecting a severe decline, the

trader expected that we would for the next few months have a market that would be a "trading market," one that would fluctuate mildly. The ability to use an option to trade against can be quite profitable to the holder, for many trades can be made against the same option, and each time a trade is made, that trade is fully protected against unlimited loss if the trader's judgment should be wrong. For example, let us say that a man buys a Put option on 100 shares at the current market price of 50 for 90 days for $350. In a few days the stock declines to 46, and the trader, feeling that the drop has been enough for the moment, buys 100 shares at 46 through this stock-broker. He must deposit the normal margin required for such a purchase as *the option cannot be used for margin.* In making such a purchase, he is guaranteed against loss because the holder of the Put option can, up until the expiration of the Put contract, deliver his stock at 50 at his option. Now he is holding 100 shares which cost 46, and since his Put option guarantees that he can sell it at 50, he is assured of no loss. Say that in the next week or so the market rallies and the stock rises to 51 and the trader decides to sell. To recapitulate: the trader bought stock at 46 and sold it at 51, yet he still retains his Put option, which does not expire for some 70 days. He has made a gross profit of five points and may have further opportunity of making additional trades—*and each time he buys stock under the price of his Put during the life of his option contract, he is guaranteed against loss.*

After having bought stock at 46 and sold it at 51, the same trader might, if the stock declines again, have another opportunity to buy more of it and, after another rally, have another chance to take a profit. The number of opportunities to make such trades is limited only by the fluctuation of the stock in the market and the trader's ability to judge the stock's movements. The reader should realize that it might be possible to make many such trades during the life of an option. Note that a trade or trades against an option do not nullify the option contract. The contract is operable until it expires or is exercised.

Buying a Put Option to Protect a Profit

A man owns 100 shares of stock which he bought at 30 four months ago. Now the stock is selling at 50. Concerned about conditions but feeling that his stock can do still better, he buys a Put contract at 50, good for 90 days, for $350. I would like to call the attention of the reader to the fact that the $350 paid for the protective Put can easily be more than made up by the fluctuations of the stock in the next 90 days.

Suppose that when the Put option expires, the stock has declined to 30. Without the protection of the Put option, the man's profit would have been lost, but through the terms of his Put contract he delivers his stock at 50 to the maker of the option. The 20 points that he has saved through the use of his Put has certainly more than paid for the cost of the option. He can, if he cares to, now repurchase at 30 the stock that he sold at 50 through exercising his Put option.

On the other hand, let us suppose that when the Put expires, the stock has advanced to 70. While the buyer then allows his option to expire (he wouldn't Put stock at 50 when he can sell it in the market at 70) the 20 points appreciation in the stock has more than made up the cost of the Put. Only if the stock is at about the same price of 50 when the option expires will the $350 paid for the contract be an actual loss. Even then it must be admitted that the Put has furnished protection during the period of the option.

Note that the holder of an option will and should exercise his contract even if the exercise will return to him *only part* of the cost. If the holder of a Put at 50 finds that at expiration the stock is selling at 48, or even 49, the contract should be exercised so as to recover part of the premium instead of losing all of it.

Bought Put at 50—cost $350
Sold Stock at 50 by exercising Put $5,000
Bought Stock in market at 48 4,800
Profit on Stock........ $ 200
Loss between profit on stock & cost of Put Option.. $ 150

An option should be exercised even if only part of its cost can be salvaged.

Buying a Put Option to Protect an Initial Commitment

Feeling bullish on a stock, a man wants to buy 100 shares but does not want to assume a big risk. He buys 100 shares at 50 and at the same time buys a Put option at 50, good for 90 days, at a cost of $350. Through the protection of his option, he knows that he can share in any rise of the stock but his loss will be limited to the cost of his Put contract. To be practical, let us see what happens if the stock goes up to 70, as he expects, or what happens if he is wrong and the stock goes down to 30. In the first instance he would sell out his stock at 70 and let the Put option lapse, and his account would read:

Bought 100 shares at 50 .... $5,000
Bought Put 100 shares at 50—cost 350
Total Cost $5,350
Sold 100 shares at 70 .... $7,000
Profit $1,650

This profit has been made with a risk of $350.

If he had been wrong and the stock had declined to 30, his account would have read:

Bought 100 shares at 50 .... $5,000
Bought Put 100 shares 350
Total Cost $5,350
Sold 100 shares at 50 (through Put) $5,000
Loss .... $ 350

Note that he sold his stock at 50 (at cost) through the terms of his Put contract, even though the stock had declined to and was selling at 30.

Special Tax Factors Covering Put Transactions

In the two preceding examples, the trader bought a 90-day Put option. In the first example, he was protecting an unrealized profit of 20 points (he had bought the stock at 30 and four months later, when the stock was at 50, he bought a Put at 50). In the second option he protected himself against loss on a new commitment (he bought the stock at 50 and at the same time he bought a Put at 50).

The first type of transaction brings into play a special rule of the federal income tax law; the second type of transaction brings into play an exception to that rule. The special rule states that if a taxpayer makes a short-sale of stock and (1) if at the time of making the short-sale he has held the same stock for not more than 6 months, or (2) if, while the short-sale was open, he has acquired more of the same stock, there will be two consequences:

First, any gain on closing the short-sale will be a short-term capital gain, even though the short-sale is closed by the delivery of stock that, at the time of delivery, has been held for more than 6 months.

Second, the holding period of the stock that at the time of the short-sale had been held for less than 6 months or had been acquired while the short-sale was open, starts on the day the short-sale is closed. The length of time that the stock was held before the short-sale was made and the length of time it was held while the short-sale was open are ignored.

For the purpose of applying this special rule, the acquisition of a Put is considered to be the making of a short-sale, and the exercise or the expiration of the Put is treated as the closing of a short-sale.

In the first example, the stock which had cost 30 had been held for only 4 months when the Put was bought. If the taxpayer had made a short-sale instead of buying a Put, the special rule would have become applicable. Since the acquisition of a Put, under these circumstances, is the making of a short-sale, such acquisition made the special rule applicable. If, when the Put expires, the market is 70 and the trader sells his stock at 70 at a time which is more than 6 months after the date of the acquisition of the stock, but not more than 6 months from the date on which the Put expired, his gain will be short term, despite the fact that he has actually held the stock for more than 6 months.

If the market is 50 or under at the expiration date of the Put, and he exercises the Put by delivering the stock which he bought at 30, his gain will be short term even though at the time of the delivery his stock has been held for more than 6 months.

If, however, he did not buy the Put until after his stock had been held for more than 6 months, the special rule would not apply for the reason that the conditions that bring the rule into play would not exist; i.e., the Put was not acquired at a time when stock had been held for not more than 6 months nor was any stock purchased while the Put was in force. Consequently, any gain on the sale of the stock, whether from a sale in the market (at a price above the price in the Put) or delivery upon exercise of the Put, will be long term.

If, when the trader buys a Put on *100 shares,* he has two lots of the same stock—100 shares which he has held for more than 6 months and 100 shares which he has held for *not more* than 6 months—a peculiar situation comes about. If the trader exercises the Put, he must be careful which lot of stock he delivers. If he delivers the lot which has been held for more than 6 months at the time he purchased the Put, he will have a short-term gain on the exercise of the Put; and if within 6 months of exercising the Put he sells the other lot, he will have a short-term gain on the latter sale, also.

This unusual situation comes about as follows:

The purchase of the Put is treated as the making of a short-sale for the reason that, at the time of the purchase, one lot of stock has been held for not more than 6 months.

The first of the two consequences mentioned above is that *any* gain on the closing of a short-sale to which the special rule applies is to be treated as a short-term gain. The second consequence is that the holding period on the stock which has been held for not more than 6 months when the Put was purchased, *starts* on the day the short-sale was closed (i.e., the day the Put was exercised). Therefore, if the latter lot is sold within 6 months of the date of the exercise of the Put, the gain will be short term.

If the trader had exercised the Put by delivering the lot which had been held for *not more* than 6 months at the time of the purchase of the Put, the gain on the closing of the short-sale would still be short term but he would be left with the lot that had been held for more than 6 months; this lot would not have lost its holding period, and when it was later sold, the gain would be long-term.

Purchasing a Put Option to Maintain a Short Position

A man is "short" of 100 shares of XYZ which he sold short at 55 (he hopes to buy it back at 30)—the stock is now selling at 50. He originally deposited funds with his broker to margin this short sale but he now has use for these funds. How can he withdraw these funds from his account and still profit by a further decline of the stock? If he covers the stock that is short, he will no longer need margin for that short sale, and he can withdraw his funds. He then buys a Put option at 50 (the market) for 90 days for $350.00. If before the expiration of the Put option the stock declines to 30, he buys stock in the market at 30 and delivers it against his Put contract at 50. He has accomplished two things—he released the margin that he needed for his business or something else and through his Put contract was able to share in the further decline in the market—all with the risk limited to the cost of the option. This operation brings to mind the oft quoted adage: You can't have your cake and eat it—but in this case you can.

Buying Stock to Make a Long-Term Gain and Protecting the Commitment

An exception to the rule that the acquisition of a Put is a short sale occurs when (1) the stock and Put are acquired on the same date, and (2) the stock is identified as that intended to be used in exercising the Put. If these two requirements are met, the acquisition of the Put will *not* be treated as a short sale and the special rule will not be applicable.

In order to get a long-term gain and have protection against loss for the entire holding period, you must buy a Put good for more than 6 months and you must buy it the same day you buy the stock.

In other words, if the stock is selling at 50 and you buy 100 shares of stock at 50 and at the same time (that is, the same day) buy a Put good for over 6 months, you are allowed to carry the stock fully protected by the Put for the duration of the option (of course, the stock must be properly margined). If at the end of 6 months and a few days the stock has risen to, say, 75, you can sell out your stock, and your profit is long-term gain. In this case, the holding period of the stock is not affected by the purchase of the protective Put option.

If, on the other hand, by the expiration of the Put the stock has declined to 30, you exercise your Put at 50, and your loss is limited to the cost of your Put option plus stock-exchange commissions and taxes. In this case you have had an opportunity to make an *unlimited long-term gain* with a risk limited to the cost of your option and commissions. How else could you have an opportunity to make a possible unlimited profit with a small limited loss?

A Put Option vs. a "Stop-Loss" Order to Protect a Purchase

Mr. A. buys 100 shares of stock at 50 and protects the purchase by buying a 90-day Put at 50, for which he pays $350. In the first 20 days, the stock declines to 45. Mr. A. doesn't have to worry—his Put option guarantees that he can sell the stock at 50 at any time before the Put contract expires—so he waits. In the next 30 or 40 days (his Put option hasn't yet expired) the stock rises to 60, and at this price Mr. A. sells his stock. He has a profit of 10 points less $350—the cost of his Put option.

Mr. B., on the other hand, buys 100 shares at 50 and at the same time enters a "stop loss" order at 46. Such an order becomes an order to sell *only* if the stock sells at 46, and then it becomes an order to sell *at the best price obtainable*. If such an order is executed or "touched off," Mr. B. will probably get 46 or less for his stock—a loss of about $400 and he is *out*. His loss is greater than the cost of the Put option which Mr. A. bought, and he cannot benefit when the stock rises to 60. See the difference?

Using a Put to Make a Long-Term Gain in a Declining Market

There is no way, except for the one I shall describe, that one can make a long-term gain in a declining market. If one has a profit on a short-sale, that profit is a *short-term gain* regardless of how long one is "short" the stock. If, in anticipation of a decline, one sold "short" at 50 and stayed short for 6 months, or even a year, and then covered at a profit, that profit would be a short-term gain. The only way that a long-term profit can be made in a falling market is through the purchase of a Put option good for over 6 months and the sale of the contract itself after it has been held over 6 months if the decline in the stock in question is great enough to show a profit. As an example:

A taxpayer buys a Put option at 50, good for 6 months and 10 days, for $500. After he has owned the option for 6 months and a day, the stock is selling at 30. By selling the actual contract to someone (and my firm—and others as well—will always be willing to buy an option from the holder which shows him a profit, if it is in our hands 24 hours before it expires) he will be selling a contract which he has held for over 6 months and the profit will be a long-term capital gain. The option-dealer will exercise the contract for his account and will sell the corresponding stock in the market (in the case of the Call), or will buy the stock in the market (in the case of a Put). The purchase price which the option-dealer will pay will be equal to the net proceeds of the dealer's transactions less two regular stock exchange commissions and any applicable tax.

You can, however, very easily spoil your opportunity to make such a long-term gain by handling such a situation wrongly; then, instead of creating a long-term gain taxable at 25 per cent, you might end up paying a tax of 60, 70, or 80 per cent according to your tax bracket. Suppose, instead of selling the Put contract for the difference between the Put price of 50 and the market price of 30, you bought the 100 shares of stock in the market at 30 and exercised your option at 50. Your profit would be the same as in the first operation, but your tax would be a short-term gain. The reason? Your tax is based not on the duration of the option but on the length of time you hold the stock in question, and in this case you would have held the stock and sold it through your Put option all in one day. This makes the difference between your paying a tax of 25 per cent or one of 60, 70, or 80 per cent, according to the tax bracket you are in.

How Option Orders Originate

Before going into the further explanation and application of options, it might be interesting to explain how orders for options originate and are executed. An interested

Explanation of Chart

U.S. STEEL

A look at the accompanying chart of U.S. Steel common shows that it broke from 72 in the second week of July, 1957, to 48¼ by the third week in December of the same year. From 48¼ it rose in almost a straight move to just under 100 in January, 1959.

In the examples that I use as illustration, people might say that I am using only favorable ones. I am using not only examples of options that were profitable to the buyer but also those where the buyer of the option was wrong and lost his premium money. Some of the examples are taken right from the records and are options that were actually sold at the time and at the price mentioned.

On July 23, 1957, when U.S. Steel was selling at 70½, 6-month-and-10-day Puts were sold at 70½ for $475 per 100-share Put. The Puts expired on February 3, 1958, and on that date the stock sold at 56. The Put contracts could have been closed out on that date with a profit of $1,450, less the cost of the option and commissions for buying and selling the stock. Of course, during the life of the option, the stock sold for as little as 48¼. Had the holder of the option seen fit to close out his option in mid-December, he could have bought stock at 49 and exercised his option before expiration, showing a profit of $2,150. Even if the man's judgment of the market had been wrong—but it wasn't—his loss would have been limited to the cost of the Put option.

If someone had been farsighted enough to buy Calls on U.S. Steel in mid-April, 1958, when steel was selling at 56, his profit could have been enormous. On April 16, 1958, Calls were sold at 57⅝, expiring in 6 months and 10 days (October 27, 1958), for $450 per 100-share Call. On October 27 the stock sold at 87, and if the Call had been closed out on that date, the profit would have been $2,937.50, less the cost of the option and stock-exchange commissions for buying and selling the stock. The owner of such a Call does not necessarily have to sell the stock after he Calls it—he may see fit to Call it and carry the stock, looking for a higher price at which to sell it. Of course, in calling the stock and carrying it, he will be required to margin the stock properly with his stock-exchange house.

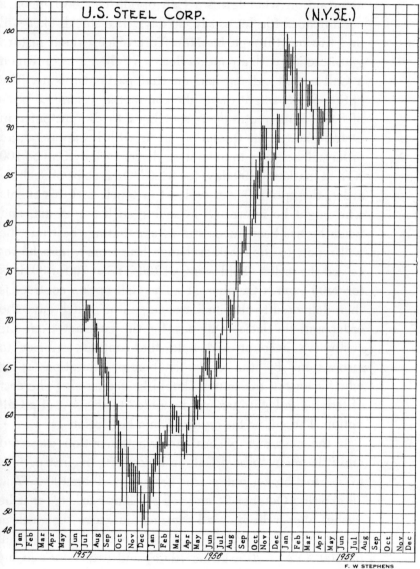

U.S. STEEL CORP. (N.Y.S.E.)

party—perhaps in Detroit—will ask his stockbroker to ascertain on what terms a Call option can be had on a certain stock for, let us say, 90 days. The stockbroker will find this out through his New York office, which in turn gets in touch with an option-dealer for the terms on which a Call option can be had on that particular issue. The option-dealer might quote the contract at a nominal price of $400. This quotation is sent back to the customer in Detroit, and if the quotation meets with his approval, an order will be given to the option-dealer to "buy Call on 100 XYZ at market for 90 days for $400." On receipt of such an order, the option-dealer will get in touch with his clients who might be interested in selling such a contract, and when he has been successful in negotiating the trade, he will report to the stock-exchange firm from whom he received the order: "Sold you Call 100 XYZ at 70 for 90 days for $400 expires October 24." The Call option contract is then delivered to the stock-exchange firm which gave the order and the latter will pay for the contract from the customer's account and hold the contract, subject to instructions by the customer before expiration as to whether or not the option should be exercised. (The cost of federal and state tax will be added to the cost of a Call option. There is no tax required on a Put option.)

If the customer wishes to have the option exercised and it happens to be a Call on XYZ at 70, his instructions to his stockbroker will read: "Exercise Call on 100 XYZ at 70 expiring October 24 and sell stock at market;" or if he wishes to exercise his Call contract and carry the stock in his account his instructions should read: "Exercise Call on 100 XYZ at 70 expiring [date] and carry stock in my account."

Of course, if he chooses to carry the stock, he will be obliged to margin it according to stock-exchange requirements. If he exercises the Call and at the same time sells the stock, he will be required to deposit only 25 per cent margin or $1000, whichever is greater.

It might be of interest at this time to explain that the option-dealer does not operate on a commission basis, but his profit is made in the difference between what he pays for an option and what he receives for it. An option-dealer having an order to buy an option for $500 will probably bid $450 to the maker of the option which he is going to sell for $500, and therefore make about $50 on the transaction. It may be possible sometimes to buy the option for a lesser amount, and in that case the option-dealer's profit will be larger. Conversely, the broker may not be able to buy the option for less than $475 in order to fill his order, and therefore his profit would be $25. So much for the various uses of the Put contract.

Uses of the Call Option Contract

A Call option is a contract, paid for when it is purchased, which gives the holder the right to buy, *at his option*, a specified number of shares of a stated stock at a fixed price, *on or before* a fixed date. The option money is the amount paid for the option contract. Should the option be exercised, it is not applied against the purchase price of the stock. If you pay $500 for a Call on XYZ at 70 and you exercise the Call, you pay 70 for the stock, less any dividends or rights that belong to the contract.

The Use of a Call Contract for Speculation

A man thinks that a stock, now selling in the market at

50, is going to have a substantial rise. He buys a Call option on 100 shares at 50, good for 90 days, for $350 plus tax. The federal and state tax departments demand that tax stamps be affixed to Call options (but not to Puts). This tax, paid for by the buyer of the option at the time he buys it, is the same amount that would be paid by a seller on a sale of the stock at the Call price. The maximum is $12 per 100 shares and is fixed according to the dollar value of the stock involved. When the trader buys the Call option at 50, good for 90 days, for $350, this amount is the most he can lose, no matter what happens to the stock. If the trader is correct in his judgment and the stock rises to, let us say, 70, before his Call contract expires, he buys the stock by exercising his Call and sells the stock in the market at 70. His profit is $2,000 less the cost of the Call contract, and his account shows:

Bought call 100 XYZ at 50 for	$ 350	
Bought 100 shares at 50 thru Call	5,000	$5,350
Sold 100 shares at 70		$7,000
Profit		$1,650

The transaction shows a profit of almost 500 per cent of the $350 at risk.

In making such a trade, when the stock is Called and sold on the same day, the holder of the Call contract will be required to deposit margin of 25 per cent of the sale price—70—with his stock-exchange broker until the trade clears on the fourth business day following the trade.

Please remember that not only does the cost of the option constitute the total risk to the holder, but the choice of exercising the option also belongs to the holder of the contract and he will exercise his option *only* if it

60

is to his advantage to do so. The seller or maker of the contract has no choice—he must live up to the terms of the contract at the option of the holder of the contract.

Closing Out a Contract for Partial Recovery

The preceding example of a Call contract for speculation showed a handsome profit. Suppose that when a Call option at 50 was about to expire the stock was selling at 52. While the holder of the Call contract could not recover all of his premium of $350, he could, nevertheless, Call for his stock at 50 and sell it in the market at 52, so instead of losing the $350 premium, he would recover $200 of it.

His account would read:

Bought Call XYZ at 50—cost .... $ 350
Bought 100 shares a/c Call 5,000
                                                                        $5,350
Sold 100 shares in market 52 .... $5,200
                                              Loss .... $ 150

(For simplification Stock Exchange commissions have been omitted.)

Selling Stock and Buying a Call
to Maintain a Position

A man is "long" 100 shares of XYZ now selling at 50. The stock is owned outright or is held on margin, but the man needs the money in his business. However, he does not like to lose his stock position. He might consider the following: He sells his stock at 50, releasing his funds, and at the same time buys a Call option at 50 good for 90 days at a cost of $350.00. If the stock advances, he exercises his Call and thereby re-acquires his stock. He may then sell the stock that he acquired through the Call and take his

61

profit, or he may care to carry the stock at 50 which is now selling in the market at 60. If, on the other hand, the stock declines to 40, he lets the Call option expire and now he can, if it suits him, re-acquire at 40 the stock that he sold in the market at 50. Through the Call contract, he accomplished two things—he released the $5,000 that he had invested and also had control over the same number of shares for the duration of his option, and at the same price that he sold them.

The Use of a Call Contract for Trading Purposes

If one is an astute trader and the market offers the opportunities, Call options can be used quite profitably and *at all times with a limited risk.*

Suppose a trader bought a 90-day Call option at the current market price of 50, for which he paid $350, and that the contract was to expire on December 31. Let us also suppose that some time in October the stock rose to 55, at which point the trader sold short 100 shares. This *short-sale*—and it must be sold as "short" stock—must be margined with his stock-exchange broker, but at this point the trade is *riskless.* The trader has a 5-point profit less the cost of the Call at any time that he cares to exercise his option. But he doesn't care to exercise his option because it has about 2 months to run and the fluctuations in the market price of the stock in that 2-month period may give him additional opportunities to trade. Let us say that after having made the short-sale at 55, the market declines in another week or so to 50, where Mr. Trader sees fit to buy in or cover his short-sale. His account now looks like this:

Sold 100 shares at 55	$5,500	
Bought 100 shares at 50		$5,000
Cost of Call Option		350
	Total Cost	$5,350
	Profit	$ 150

But the Call runs until December 31, and the trade which was made does not nullify the option. In another week or so, because of some news, the stock rallies to 56, where Mr. Trader again sees fit to sell short. Again he has a riskless, profitable transaction, and in a week or so the stock again declines to 50, at which point the short-sale is covered. On this trade another profit of $600 is added to the $150 already made.

Sold 100 shares at 56	$5,600	
Bought 100 shares at 50		5,000
	Profit	$ 600

Past performances of many stocks show that such opportunities are far from rare and there have been instances of as many as twelve full trades made against a Call before its expiration. Without owning the Call, Mr. Trader might have been fearful of making a short-sale but, knowing that he could always cover the short-sale at 50 through the terms of his Call contract, he does not hesitate to trade. Suppose, for argument's sake, that after having made the short-sale at 56, the stock advances to 70 and stays at about that price. The trader merely exercises his call, thereby covering at 50, through the terms of his contract, the short-sale that he made at 56. Without the Call option he would have a 14-point loss, and even though the short-sale would prove to be a bad trade, his *guaranteed trade* would show a profit. Just as a Call can be used to protect a trade for trading purpose, Call options can also be used to:

Protect a Short-Sale at Time of Commitment

A man feels that a stock now selling at 50 will decline and sells 100 shares short in the market. Not willing to risk an unlimited loss if the stock advances, he buys a Call option at 50, good for 90 days, for which he pays $350. He is now guaranteed through the terms of his Call that he can buy 100 shares at 50 *at his option* before the contract expires, so if he is wrong, his loss will be limited to the cost of his Call option.

Now let's look at the operation both ways: Let's see what happens if the man is right and the stock declines and if he is wrong and the stock goes up instead of down. If the stock should go down to 30, as the man expects, he covers his stock in the market at 30 and takes his 20-point profit. Naturally, he won't want to exercise his Call option to buy stock at 50 because he can buy it better in the market, so he allows his Call option to lapse. He:

Sold 100 shares at 50	$5,000	
Bought 100 shares at 30		$3,000
Bought Call at 50		350
		$3,350
Profit		$1,650

One might say that he could have made the short-sale without having spent $350 for the protection. Certainly— but suppose that instead of the stock going down to 30, it had gone to 55, 60, 65, and then 70. What then? How far do you let your loss run? Well, some would say, why not sell the stock short and put a "stop loss" order in at 53½?

If the stock declined to 30, he would have saved the $350 and his profit would have been $2,000 instead of $1,650. That's fine, but suppose the stock rose to 54 first, stopped out the man's short-sale with a loss of $350 or $400, and then declined to 30. His original idea was correct—the stock did decline to 30—but the stop-loss order for protection was more costly than the Call option. If he had had the Call option, the rally to 54 would not have worried him because he would have been guaranteed through his contract that he could cover at 50, but the stop-loss order caused him a quick and definite loss.

The Use of a Call Option to Average

Those who remember the market decline in late 1957 and the middle of 1962 recall that people who had bought stocks at high prices before the decline did not have much desire for or even spare funds, for that matter, to try to average their costs by buying additional shares. If a man had bought a stock at 40 and found it selling at 20 a few months later (many stocks did that), he didn't have much incentive to buy additional shares. Had he known the technique of averaging through the purchase of Call options, he might have done well.

Suppose that, after the fall from 40 to 20, the man inquired and learned that he could buy Call options at 20 good for 90 days for $225 per 100-share Call. Now it doesn't take as much nerve—or as much money—to buy a Call for $225 as it would to buy another hundred shares of stock for $2,000. If Mr. Trader (or call him Mr. Investor) had bought such a Call at 20, and before the expiration the stock had advanced to 35, and at that point

65

he sold both the stock that had cost him 40 and the stock that had cost him 20, which he had on Call, his account would look like this:

Bought 100 shares at 40 .... $4,000
Bought Call 100 shares at 20 225
Bought 100 shares at 20 a/c Call 2,000
$6,225

Sold 200 shares at 35 .... $7,000

Profit .... $ 775

On the other hand—and we like to look at both sides—had he not bought the Call, a rise of 35 in the stock would have left him with a 5-point loss on his original stock. Instead, by the additional risk of $225, the rise to 35 gave him the opportunity to come out with a profit.

Protect Profit in a Call by Buying a Put

Here's a tricky one but very useful. A man bought a 90-day Call at 50 (stock was selling at 50) for $350. In 60 days the stock rose to 70. At this price of 70 he has a 20-point profit, less the cost of his option, and he buys a 60-day Put at 70 for about $400. Let us see what happens. Say that in the 60-day life of his Put the stock declines again to 50. He has lost the profit that he had on his Call, but he has a 20-point profit on his Put, less 2 premiums totaling $750—a net gain of $1,250.

Or, say that in the remaining 30 days of his Call, the stock continues to rise and goes to 80. He then has a profit of $3,000 less the two premiums of $750, or a net profit of $2,250. This treatment can be varied by the purchase of two Puts instead of one.

The uses of options are limited only by one's ability and ingenuity.

Buying Stock and Call at the Same Time

There is a theory among some traders that, if they are bullish enough on a stock to buy a Call, they should be bullish enough to buy stock at the same time with the idea that, if the stock advances to a point where the profit will pay the cost of the Call contract, they can sell the stock and have the Call for nothing.

A stock is selling at 50. and the man buys a Call at 50 on 100 shares for 90 days for $350. At the same time, he buys 100 shares in the market at 50 (which he must margin). If the stock advances to 55 in a few weeks and he sells his stock, he has made $500, less commission, which will about pay for the Call option. Now he has his Call option at 50; the stock is selling at 55 and the Call cost him nothing, with some time for the Call still to run. From here until the time the contract expires, he may trade to his heart's content above the Call price for he has his Call as protection. He may sell short at 60, cover at a lower price, then sell again and cover again as long as there is a profit. If the stock goes up after a short sale, he can always use his Call to cover his short sale.

Trading in Odd Lots Against a Call

Personally, I don't approve of trading like this—I believe in going whole hog—but there are some who like to scale their orders to sell against an option which they hold. For instance, take a man who owns a Call option on 100 shares at 50, good for 90 days, for which he paid $350; his idea of trading is to sell 50 shares short at 60, and maybe

Explanation of Chart

CHRYSLER

Take, for example, a man who bought 100 Chrysler on August 20, 1957, at 80. By November 20 (or in 90 days) he would have had a loss of $1,400, and in 6 months his loss would have been $3,000. Compare his position with that of a man who bought a 90-day Call contract on 100 Chrysler at 80 on August 20, at the market for $500. Let us suppose also that this last man bought a 6-month Call at 80 on August 20 for which he paid $750. Neither the 90-day Call nor the 6-month Call would have shown a profit. The man who bought the Call options was as wrong in his market judgment as the first man, and he lost the money that he paid for the Calls—but that money was the limit of his risk. Now, after Chrysler declined, the man who had bought the Calls instead of the stock and had drawn from the equity in his account only the cost of the Call contract, was in a position to buy the actual stock at a much lower price than when he first became bullish on it. Even though the purchase of the Calls was unprofitable, it saved him from buying the stock at the original high price.

As another example, suppose a man was bullish on Chrysler in the third week in July, 1958. The stock, according to the chart, sold at 46½. At that time he could have bought a 90-day Call contract at 46½ (the price at which it was selling) for $350. During the life of the Call the stock advanced, and in the third week in October, when his Call expired, the stock sold at 58. He could have exercised his Call at 46½ and at the same time sold the stock at 58, thereby making approximately 11½ points, less the cost of his option and commission for buying and selling the stock.

The records show also that 6-month-and-10-day Calls were bought on October 24, 1958, at 53½ for $600 per 100-share Call, when the stock was selling at that price. On May 4, 1959, when the Call expired, the stock was selling at 68, showing a profit of $1,450, less the cost of the Call and stock-exchange commissions for buying and selling the stock.

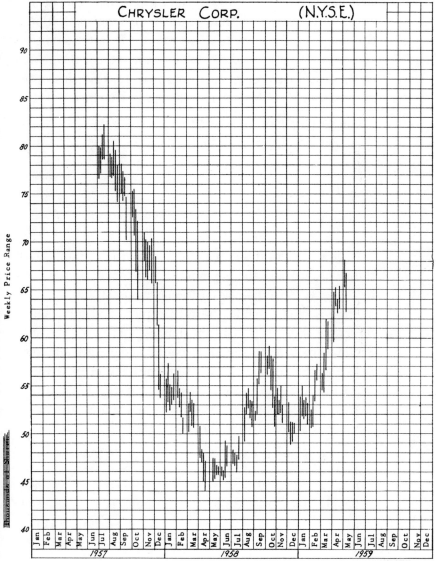

CHRYSLER CORP.   (N.Y.S.E.)

Weekly Price Range

1957   1958   1959

F. W. STEPHENS
. 87 NASSAU STREET, NEW YORK 38, N. Y.
TEL. BEEKMAN 3-9090

50 shares short at 65. Of course, he must deposit margin with his stockbroker to take such a position, and he may be able to trade back and forth before the expiration of the option and complete many trades. If, after selling 50 shares short at 60 and 50 shares short at 65, the market continues to rise to 70 or 75, he just exercises his option at expiration and his account will look like this:

Bought Call 100 shares at 50	$ 350	
Bought 100 shares at 50 through Call	5,000	
	$5,350	
Sold 50 shares at 60		$3,000
Sold 50 shares at 65		3,250
Total proceeds		$6,250
Profit		$ 900

Notice the profit against the cost of the option (notice the leverage) and the percentage gain; at no time was the risk greater than the cost of the option contract.

Suppose that, before the Call expires and after selling 50 shares short at 60 and 50 shares short at 65, the stock declines to 45. At this point it would be more advantageous to the trader to buy the stock in the market to cover his short-sale than to exercise his Call option. He buys 100 shares at 45 to cover his short-sale and allows his Call to lapse. His account then looks like this:

Sold 50 shares at 65	$3,250	
Sold 50 shares at 60	3,000	
Bought Call at 50		$ 350
Bought 100 shares at 45		4,500
	$6,250	$4,850
Profit		$1,400

Buying Long-Term Calls for Tax Benefit

The idea in finance today is to make money, true; but *how much* money net? What's left *after* tax? For that reason people look for long-term capital gains on which the tax is 25 per cent maximum. A man in the upper income tax bracket may have to pay a tax of 75 per cent or 80 per cent on his ordinary income, but the same amount of long-term capital gain calls for a maximum tax of 25 per cent. Instead of making a dollar, paying 75 cents in tax, and having 25 cents left, one is better off making only 50 cents on a long-term capital-gains basis, paying 12½ cents, and having 37½ cents left. Therefore, in any form of capital asset, people look for capital gains opportunities.

In the securities market we know that to buy shares and hold them for *over* 6 months and make a profit creates a gain taxable at 25 per cent maximum. A profit made in less than 6 months is *short*-term profit, taxable at the same rate as ordinary income. To buy 100 shares of stock at 50 may result in a gain either long- or short-term—or it may result in a loss. And we don't know how much loss there may be. The Call option for over 6 months—usually for 6 months and 10 days—offers an unlimited possible gain and a *limited* risk. The risk is limited to the cost of the Call option contract.

The following illustrates this. A man who expects a stock which is selling at 50 to rise, buys a Call option at 50, good for 6 months and 10 days, for $500. Notice the price of $500 for a 6-month option as compared to a 90-day contract for $350. The proportion is about like that—double the length of the contract for about 50 per cent more. If

71

the expected rise materializes and the stock goes to, say, 70 after Mr. Trader has held the contract *for over* **6** months, he *sells* his Call contract *instead of exercising it.* We (and most option-dealers) will always be interested in buying a profitable option; in such instances, we will purchase the Call and exercise it for our own account (50), and sell the stock in the market (70) for our own account. The purchase price which we will pay for the Call will be equal to our net proceeds ($2,000.00), less two regular stock exchange commissions and any applicable tax. In selling such a contract, it has not been necessary to deposit margin with the option-dealer. It is my understanding that, in such transactions, the selling option-holder has ordinarily treated the profit as long term capital gain on the sale of a contract held for more than six months.

It must be carefully noted, however, that if the holder of the contract *exercises* his option at 50 and at the same time sells the stock in the market at 70, such a profit is *short-term gain* by reason of the fact that the stock was held only one day. The holding period of the stock in this case does not date back to the time of the purchase of the option, but only to the time of actual acquisition of the stock.

Compare the two types of trades:

Bought Call at 50	$ 500
Sold Call at 50 with stock 70	2,000
Long-Term Profit	$1,500

The tax on this would be 25 per cent or $375, leaving a profit *after* tax of $1,125.

If the Call had been exercised and the stock sold in the market on the same day, the account would read as follows:

Bought Call at 50 ....Cost $ 500
Bought stock at 50 by exercise of Call.... 5,000

Sold stock in market at 70 .... $7,000
                    Short-Term Gain....... $1,500

If this man's income put him in the 75 per cent bracket, he would pay $1,125 in tax and be left with only $375 net profit *after* tax. While this procedure is extremely interesting, so is the action taken by the holder of an option that proves unprofitable. If the 6-month option is allowed to lapse, the loss—the cost of the option—is a long-term capital loss. A loss was sustained on a contract which was held *over* 6 months. However, if the contract which looks as if it will be a loss is sold to another for a nominal sum before the contract is held for 6 months—say 5 months and 20 days, or anything up to 6 months—the loss is a short-term loss.

Bought Call at 50 .... $500
Sold Call 1
                Loss $499

Such short-term losses are valuable to the trader who might have short-term gains, for short-term losses are applicable against short-term profits.

Let us say that a trader has a short-term profit in securities or any capital asset of $500. He buys a Call option of two different stocks for $500 each. One Call is a loss, and he sells the contract in less than 6 months for $1. The other Call is profitable and he sells the contract after 6 months for $2,000 less the cost of his contract—$500. His result is a $1,500 long-term gain on the sale of one contract, and a short-term loss of $499 on the sale of the other contract. The $499 loss practically wipes out the $500 short-term profit and leaves an over-all long-term gain of $1,500, taxable at 25 per cent. Traders in securities would do well to understand this procedure.

As a side thought I would like to tell this story. It happened in November, 1957, after the market had had a severe break. A man with a southern drawl and wearing a big ten-gallon hat, walked into our office and wanted to speak to the "boss." "You know," he said, "I bought a lot of your Calls and I tore them up—lost my money." I thought maybe he was going to pull a gun on me. But my fear quickly vanished when he said, "Don't worry—how lucky it was that I bought Calls instead of stock. If I had bought the stocks way up there I would have gone broke." (The Dow Jones averages declined from 520 in July, 1957, to 420 in October.)

To buy an option, either a Put or a Call, and be wrong, can result in the loss of the cost of the option—that's all. But to buy a stock or sell a stock short and be wrong can cost a lot of money.

The Renewal of Options

Options can very often be extended. Suppose you own a Call contract at 54 on a stock which has risen before the expiration of the option to 65. You feel that if you had more time, the stock could go higher—to 75, 80, or more—in another 60 or 90 days. Through your stock-exchange house or your option-dealer, arrangements may be made for an extension of the contract. The cost of an extension, if it can be made, depends on many things: the option price, the price of the stock in the market, the length of time of the extension, and, of course, the willingness of the original maker of the contract to extend the option.

The Exercise of Options Before Expiration

Just because one holds a Call or a Put option for 90 days is no reason to wait until the last of the option time to act upon it. Many times a stock will rise considerably above the Call price or decline much below the Put price during the time of the option, but the holder of the option who does not take timely advantage of the situation may find that at the expiration most of the profit that *had been* in the contract has disappeared. For example, the holder of a Call contract at 50 having 20 days left out of a 90-day contract, finds the stock selling at 65, at which price he would have a nice profit if he would close out the contract. But he waits until the last day or near the last day, by which time the stock has declined to 54, wiping out most or all of the profit. A contract can be exercised *at any time* before the contract expires.

The Effect of Options on the Stock Market

Consider, if you will, what effect the exercise of options or the trading against options has on prices on the exchange. The effect is to stabilize. The buyer of a Put option is not a seller of stock as is a trader who sells short. On the contrary, he is a buyer of stock and usually in a falling market. Let us consider the case of a man who, expecting the market to decline, buys a Put not on 100 shares but on

3,000 shares of a stock at 50. If the market declines to 40, and the man who owns the Put option is satisfied with such a profit, he may be a buyer of stock on a scale-down—500 at 40, 500 at 39, 500 at 38, and so on—until he has bought the 3,000 shares of stock covered by his Put option. His purchases strengthened the market on that stock.

I remember how, many years ago, a very large investor sold Put options in thousands of shares of a particular stock. The market as a whole became quite weak, but not this stock. Most of the holders of the Put options wanted to buy stock against their Puts and this action supported and stabilized the stock.

Call options also have a stabilizing effect on the market. The holder of Calls which are profitable closes them out by Calling or buying the stock which is specified in the Call contract and selling that stock in the market to complete the trade. A man who owns Call options becomes a supplier of stocks in a rising market. He sells the shares that he Calls in order to make his profit. Whether a man sells against his Calls in a rising market or buys against his Put options in a declining market, his actions are against the trend and, therefore, stabilizing and not destructive.

Effect of Dividends, Rights, and Stock Dividends

On the day that a stock sells ex a cash dividend on the exchange, the prices in all outstanding Put and Call options on that stock will be reduced automatically by the amount of the dividend. For example, the holder of a Put option and a Call option, both at 50, will, on the day that the stock sells ex dividend $1.00 on the Exchange, automatically reduce both the Put and the Call option price to 49. While the holder of actual stock would be the recipient of such a dividend when it is payable, the holder of a Call option does not receive the dividend, but reduces the price of his Call option. Conversely, one who is short actual stock when it sells ex dividend would be charged for the dividend, while the holder of a Put contract reduces the price of his contract and pays the dividend *only* in the form of the reduced price when and if he exercises his contract.

In the case of rights issued on a stock, the prices in all outstanding options are reduced by an amount equal to the price at which the first sale of the rights is made on the day that the stock sells ex rights on the Exchange. Thus, if the first sale of the rights *on the day the stock sells ex rights* is 1½, then the price of outstanding Put and Call contracts would be reduced by 1½ points. The stock at the opening on the day that the stock sells ex rights would probably open down 1½ points so that there would be no advantage to either the buyer or the seller of the options.

Suppose that one owns a Put and a Call at 52 and the company has declared a 5 per cent dividend. From the day that the stock sells ex stock dividend the holder of the Call contract, if and when he exercises his Call, calls for 105 shares of stock for $5,200 (the dollar amount specified in the original contract) and the holder of the Put option, if he exercises his Put, will deliver 105 shares for $5,200 (the total dollar amount specified in the original contract).

As an example: the holder of a Call on 100 shares of

American Motors at 20, with stock selling at 40 after it has sold ex a 5 per cent dividend, would Call for 105 shares of stock for $2,000. Conversely, the holder of a Put on American Motors at 20 if the stock were selling at 10 (after it had sold ex the 5 per cent stock dividend) would Put 105 shares of stock for the sum of $2,000. If the stock has sold ex a 50-cent cash dividend and then ex a 5 per cent stock dividend, the holder of the Call at 20 would reduce his Call price to 19½ and then Call for 105 shares for $1,950.

Percentage of Options Exercised

I can remember when I testified before the Senate Finance Committee in 1934. I was, of course, younger and less experienced, but I had been in the option business for fifteen years at that time and, although the business then was different from what it is now, I knew it well. I had already appeared before Congressman Sam Rayburn's committee in the House and now I had been selected by the Put and Call Brokers and Dealers Association to represent the industry before the Senate. There I was in a big room with a "mike" before me; the senators who were on the committee sat at a large table, and there were about three hundred spectators and witnesses in the room. I was facing Senator Fletcher, Ferdinand Pecora, Ben Cohen, and "Tom" Corcoran—the framers of the Securities Act. "Tom the Cork," as Mr. Corcoran was called, had explained the bill, paragraph by paragraph, and when he came to the part dealing with options, he said, in substance, "Not knowing the difference between good options and bad options, for the matter of convenience we strike them all out." Don't hold me to the exact words, but that was the essence of it and it was my job to show the difference. I think I did a good job. As I have said, the business of options was turned over to the newly formed SEC and, sitting before this body, I explained the difference between "the options in which we deal which are publicly offered and openly sold for a consideration, and the manipulative options that had been secretly given, for no fee but for manipulative purposes."

To get back to the reason for the heading of this section, Mr. Pecora, after other questions, asked me the percentage of options that were exercised, and I told him that about 12½ per cent were exercised at or before expiration. Remember that in those days options were mostly of 30-day duration written not "at the market" price, but away from the market. In those days we also negotiated options for 2 days, 7 days, and 15 days. (More about this later.) But stock prices were high in the twenties (as we later found out), and with General Motors over $300, U.S. Steel over $325, and many stock in the hundreds, it was quite common to trade options 20, 30, or even 40 points away from the market for 30 days.

Mr. Pecora then asked something like this: "If only 12½ per cent are exercised, then the other 87½ per cent of the people who bought options have thrown their money away?" "No, sir," I said, "if you insured your house against fire and it didn't burn down you would not say that you had thrown away your insurance premium."

The same thing is true about options. Today the 30-day

option is a very small percentage of our business, and the longer contracts in which we now deal constitute a very much greater percentage of options exercised. However, whether an option is exercised at expiration or not, it does supply considerable protection and advantage to the holder during its life.

Just one short example: A man owns stock that cost him 40 and is now selling at 70. He protects that profit with a 90-day Put at 70, for which he pays $400. During the life of the option, the stock advances to 80, and Mr. Trader allows his Put option to lapse. Instead of his selling his stock at 70, the protection afforded by the Put provides him with the incentive or courage to hold the stock for an additional 10 points profit without risking the profit he already has. The option isn't exercised, but would you say that Mr. Trader "threw away" the premium that he paid for the Put option, or did he have protection during the life of his option for his full profit and against an unlimited loss?

"Years Ago"

It might be interesting to the reader at this point, after reading so much of the techniques of the option business, to know something of "years ago."

When I first came into the option business forty years ago, and up until about the time of the "big break" in 1929, the holder of an option could trade against it with no margin. His broker had to have coverage for just the commissions and interest and any market difference. Often I had Puts on 500 shares against which I would trade, back and forth, as many times as the swings in the market would allow; margin was not necessary because the option, guaranteed by a member firm of the New York Stock Exchange, was sufficient margin. Not so today, however. Today all stock commitments must be covered by the required margin and the option is not a substitute for such margin.

"Years ago," Spreads and Straddles were sold so that the exercise of one side of the option, before expiration, voided the other side of the contract. The Straddle was made out as one contract and the contract was surrendered to exercise one side.

"Years ago," there were no tax stamps required on either the Put or the Call option.

"Years ago," contracts were made out in 500 or 1,000 shares, or even in 5,000-share pieces, instead of in single 100-share pieces as they are today. The largest trades I ever made were some 25,000-share pieces, but 5,000-share trades were common. The largest trade I remember was an order I had for Call options on 5,000 shares each on 22 different stocks. The order was filled without too much trouble in about 3 days.

"Years ago," very few option-dealers had their own offices. The "market" was in a restaurant in New Street, New York City, where most of the option-dealers congregated, and many large writers and buyers of options would come to meet with their special option-dealers and give an order. There were telephone booths and a ticker in the restaurant, and the telephone booths were our offices. All the dealers walked around with a pocketful of nickels, ready to use a phone to call a customer and try to make a trade. (A phone call was still a nickel in those days). Of course, we all ate in that restaurant—we had to, for a customer might call and this was our "office."

"Years ago," we did a very large business in "2-day options." We bought them for $25 or $30 per hundred and sold them for $35 or $37.50. They ran from, say, Monday—that would be at any time Monday that we traded—until Wednesday at 2:45 P.M.—the Exchange closed at 3:00 P.M. in those days. We would buy Calls on some stock 2, 3, 5, 10, or 20 points above the market for 2 days. But the number of points demanded for a Call was in proportion to the way the stocks were moving. And if you knew which pool was going to move which stock in the next 2 days, you could do well. There was a broker in the business who would sell a Call on 100 shares of stock good, for the next day only, for one dollar's worth of cigars (which were seven for a dollar, then). The idea was to buy one of those "seven-cigar Calls" and about noon the next day, if the stock had had a run, to sell it for $25 or more—just for the rest of the day. I saw one of my colleagues make $1,200 on a call like that.

All of the brokers would congregate in the restaurant after the close of the market to "chew the rag." There was one fellow who would sell lists—100-share Calls on, say, seven different stocks at a price above the close with the Calls good for the next day—and he might offer the whole list for $25 or $50, according to the list of stocks. Very often, before noon the next day, the buyer of the list sold *one* of the Calls for $100. Fluctuations were wide in those days and stocks weren't split so quickly. Some of the leading stocks sold over $300—General Motors, Mexican Petroleum, Texas Company moved 10–20–30 points in a day. I remember selling a man Puts on General Motors and Mexican Petroleum 30 points below the market for 30 days. Those Puts cost $137.50 per hundred shares, but the next day or so those stocks were down 40 points and the next day they were up 30. I sold a fellow a Call on Radio once for 30 days at 100—the stock was 89 and the Call cost $137.50. There were 100 points in the Call when it was exercised.

"Years ago," there were two individuals in the street—not Put and Call brokers exactly—who traded for their own account. They bought Spreads—they would buy a Spread on 500 Studebaker selling at 80—Puts at 72, and Calls at 90, for 30 days for $200 per 100-share Spread. If the stock went up in a few days, they sold the Call for $200, and then if the stock declined they sold the Put for $100 or $200, according to the price of the stock. But one partner wouldn't sell a contract unless the other partner agreed, and it was funny to watch one partner run up and down New Street looking for the other to O.K. a contemplated sale of a contract. Sometimes a broker would ask to have the contract "in hand" for a few minutes to see if he could sell it. He'd disappear into a nearby brokerage office and wait to see if the stock moved and then come out to say, "O.K., I sold it."

"Years ago," I remember trading a Call on 10,000 shares of Pan American Pete at 11:00 P.M. at night. When I first started, I did the trading, I made out the contracts in ink—

who owned a typewriter?—I made out the checks, I delivered the contract, I picked up the checks and made the deposits, I opened the shop and closed the shop; I was the business. But all of the option-dealers did very well. After a while I chipped in with another broker and we hired a boy for $15 a week to stand at some phone booths in a nearby building (these phone booths were our branch office), and if we were wanted on the phones down the street our boy would come running after one of us "big shots" and whoever was wanted would run up to answer "his" phone. What fun if the restaurant phone wanted you at the same time!

But we had a peculiar sense of honor in those days. If I was sick for a time, one of my competitors would answer my calls and do business for me, and upon my return to work, he would give me a list of the trades he had made for me, along with a check for my profits. And though every one of us was a competitor and would try to offer an option better than the next fellow, the broker who took care of the sick fellow's customers would not, on the latter's recovery, solicit business from his fellow broker's customers. It just wasn't cricket. I had pneumonia once after I had been in business about four years. At the time I was trying to follow a buying pool—only I didn't know that it was selling in another place. I lost my money and worried about my wife and kid, and got sick and contracted pneumonia. I was home for about four weeks, but one of my competitors took care of my business and wouldn't take more than a "thank you" for it.

While I still had my office in my hat—I mean the

restaurant—I made a trade in 500 shares with an English fellow I had seen around "the shop," and as he said, "I'll take it," he winked his eye. Trying to be careful because I couldn't afford to make a mistake, I asked him again if it was a trade and again he said, "I'll take it," but gave another wink. I went over to one of the boys and asked him about this fellow, who, every time he said, "I'll take it," winked at me. They reassured me that the sale was O.K.—he just had a nervous twitch—but I was scared.

Despite the length of time I've been in this business, I can remember almost all of the mistakes that were made in trading, they were that few. It's amazing because of the millions of shares of options that are traded: a Put is a Put and not a Call; 100 is 100 and not 500; and Steel is Steel and not Studebaker. I hope I don't jinx it, but I can't remember a serious mistake in our office in almost 10 years.

Just to show how mistakes were *not* made—often we would call a certain seller of options at his home at 7 P.M. (he was a fellow who had quite a thirst—so much so, that his tongue thickened) and we'd trade a thousand or two with him, and next morning our contracts would come in 100 per cent perfect—just as they had been traded. I don't think there is another business in the whole wide world that has had as few errors in the last forty years as the option business. And it's fast—we've over 50 phones on our trading table, and on a fast day the twelve ears and twelve hands that our six traders have can't stop for a minute; still, I think it should get an "Oscar" for being the least understood of all Wall Street businesses.

And speaking of "years ago," the following pages are reproductions of a few pages of a book that was given to me. The book fascinated me so much that I had a limited number of copies made, not only because it tells of the option business and the stock-exchange of those days, but because I felt it was a museum piece. The frontispiece is dated 1875. One of the sketches shows the Sub-Treasury Building at Wall and Broad Streets, New York, but there was no statue of George Washington in the picture, as there is now. I investigated and found out why: George was put there eight years after this little book was published. I have added these few pages of this little book to mine because I thought that the reader would be interested in it. I hold the original in my Wall Street "Put and Call Library" for posterity.

General Answers to Inquiries.

We have daily inquiries from correspondents at a distance, saying that living so far from the city, and not knowing the best stock to select, or the most favorable time to close their contracts, that if we would attend to not only securing the privelege, but the selection of the stock, and closing the same, using our best judgment, they would be willing to forward their money to us for investment. We reply, that when requested, we will not only secure the privilege, but make the selection of stock and the kind of contract best to be taken, and also attend to the closing of same, exercising our best judgment. We are enabled to do this without prejudice to our customers, as our business is done strictly on commission, and we are entirely disinterested when we give our views of the market, which we never do until after studying the movements of the different cliques, and watching the outside influences that may be brought to bear on the market. It is to our interest as well as our customers', to select such stocks as are most likely to pay the best profits, for as we make money for them, we make it for ourselves, by increasing our business; and all who trust us with their business may rest assured that we will attend promptly and faithfully to their interest.

We do not guarantee or promise success in every instance. We present such facts before our readers from week to week as may come into our possession, and give them our best judgment as to the probable course of the market for the ensuing thirty days, and we say to them, if you choose to risk $106.25, you may realize a considerable profit. The stock broker who buys and sells for his customers can do no more than this. If he is consulted and is candid, he will tell his client what he thinks as to the prospects of a stock, desiring him at the same time to exercise his own judgment. He does not guarantee profits or promise success by any means. Those of our patrons who have followed the course of our suggestions, will agree with us when we state that our prognostications have generally proved correct, and when they have taken our advice, success has resulted in nine cases out of ten.

We have no intention of urging people to speculate against their wishes, and we desire to be understood as saying, that any person who has money which cannot be spared, had better not risk it either in speculations on margins or with privileges. If any one feels that he would be distressed by the loss of the funds which he proposes to use in speculation, let him give Wall Street a wide berth. On the other hand, a judicious investment of a few hundred dollars in stock privileges, may be the stepping stone to fortune, and it must be remembered that one profitable venture will repay the losses on a great number of unprofitable ones. So the ball of speculation once in motion is easily kept rolling, and gains at every turn.

All orders by mail or telegraph will receive our prompt attention, and should be addressed,

TUMBRIDGE & CO.,

BANKERS AND BROKERS, 2 Wall St., N. Y.

INTERIOR VIEW OF THE BANKING HOUSE OF TUMBRIDGE & CO.

CUSTOMERS DEPARTMENT.

PRIVATE OFFICE.

WAITING ROOM.

Secret of Success in Wall Street.

Persons unacquainted with Stock Speculation may become perfectly familiar with the intricate machinery necessary for its operation by a **CAREFUL** *study of these pages. They will also attain a knowledge of financial matters useful in any pursuit, and may be the means of their making many safe and profitable investments; even those who have had an interest in stocks will find information and hints unknown to them before, which will greatly aid and increase their gains in future operations. In return we solicit a share of your patronage.*

WALL Street has been in existence since 1687. Its name was derived from the Wall or angle built on the northern line of the street to ward off the Indians, and was the scene of many a conflict, but none were more exciting than those of the present day, muscle and sinew then, but brains gain the victory now; campaigns are planned and strategy displayed on Change as well as on the tented field.

Wall Street has its dashing assaults and stout defences; its ammunition consists of a balance in the banks of three hundred million dollars; its generals reign while able to enforce obedience, and carry dismay and confusion into the enemy's camp.

The love of money is as strong as the love of dominion, and avarice, like its nobler brother ambition, scorns delights and lives laborious days. In short, the street retains all the excitement of the battle field, and yet is the entrance gate to civilization, society, honor, fame and wealth.

At the head of the street, and immediately opposite the offices of TUMBRIDGE & Co., stands Trinity Church. the chimes of whose bells marks the hour at which active business in the Gold and Stock Exchanges and the Banks commence for the day.

SUGGESTIONS.

☞ If you are undecided which way a stock is going, always take a "Spread;" it costs $212.50, and pays a profit if the stock goes up or down.

☞ To take an interest in several different stocks will generally be successful; in the numerous fluctuations which occur every day, you are certain to make a handsome profit on some of them.

☞ Where a stock has once been in price, you may look for it to sell there again at some time.

☞ **Short of Stocks.**—To be "Short of Stocks," or a "Bear," means that you have sold for a decline, stocks, which you have not in your possession, but your Broker borrows for delivery.

☞ **Long of Stocks.**—The expression being "Long of Stocks," or a "Bull," means that you have bought for a rise, and that the shares are in possession of your broker.

☞ Our long experience in stock operations gives us many advantages, and coming in contact with the great stock manipulators, we are often able to judge of the future market and give our customers very valuable information and advice, enabling them to act upon it.

☞ We are always careful to make contracts on parties of undoubted responsibility, and our customers can always obtain the name of the party from whom we have bought or sold contracts or stocks for their account.

☞ The best stocks to secure contracts on are those in which the greatest activity is anticipated. When requested, we will make the investment in such stocks as, in our judgment, will give the largest returns, and will act for parties in securing the profits.

☞ **Contracts Left With Us** we will operate against either by buying or selling, in order to secure the various fluctuations of the day. Our customers are entitled to our services in the selection of the style of investment most likely to prove profitable for their account without extra commission charges.

☞ If you think stocks are going down secure a Put; or you can obtain a Call and sell the stocks short against it.

☞ If you think stocks are going up, secure a Call, or you can obtain a Put, and buy the stock against it.

☞ When a telegraphic order is received by us and we have no funds to the credit of the person sending such order, a check on New York, payable to our order, must be received by us by first mail.

☞ We can always make returns the same day a contract is closed.

☞ Extensions or renewals must be secured before the expiration of the original contract.

☞ **No Liability.**—There is no liability, or risk, beyond the amount paid for a privilege.

☞ Register all money letters, send large amounts by express or draft on New York, and address all communications

TUMBRIDGE & CO.,

Bankers and Brokers,

2 WALL STREET, N. Y.

demand the stock. If on the other hand the stock should decline, and not advance above the price named in the Call, the
only loss that can possibly occur is the amount that may have
been paid for the contract.

An actual transaction illustrated will assist the reader. By
referring to our books we find that in March, when Union
Pacific was selling at 41, we secured calls on this stock at 43 for
30 days, the cost of which was $106.25. The following is a
copy of the contract secured :

New York, March 3d, 1875.

For Value Received, *The Bearer may CALL*
ON ME for One Hundred Shares of the Capital Stock of the
Union Pacific Railroad Company, at Forty three per cent., any
time in thirty days from date.
The Bearer is entitled to ALL DIVIDENDS OR EXTRA
DIVIDENDS paid during the time.
Expires April 2d, 1875.
1:45 P. M.   Signed.........................

Negotiated by
TUMBRIDGE & CO.,
Bankers and Brokers in Stock Privileges,
Stocks Bought and Sold on Margins.
P. O. Box 2282.   2 WALL ST.

Every one per cent. Union Pacific advances above the price
named, viz. : 43 is equal to $100 on each hundred shares, so an
advance of five per cent., the contract would be worth Five
Hundred Dollars, an advance of ten per cent. would be a thousand dollars, and so on. This is always the case. One per cent.
on a stock that is worth in the market only 15, amounts to just
as much as on a stock that is worth 110, because it is always the
par value of a stock that is referred to, and not the selling
value.

Before the above Call expired, Union Pacific had advanced to
66, at which price we closed the contract by receiving the stock
from the maker of the contract at 43, giving our check for
$4,300 and selling the stock in the market for 66, the holder
of the contract receiving the difference. A statement would be
as follows :

March 29th, 100 U. P. sold 66, less ⅛ Commissions......$6,587.50
March 29th, 100 U. P., called at 43.................... 4,300 00

$2,287.50
Deduct cash paid for Call at 43 and Commissions....... 106.25

Profit on the transaction........... .... $2,181.25

THE USE OF A PUT CONTRACT.

A PUT contract is the very reverse of a Call—the holder having the right to deliver stock to the signer of the contract at a fixed price before its expiration. The maker of the contract is the only party bound, so that when advantage is taken of the contract and a delivery of stock made, it is always profitable for the holder of the contract. Consequently the market or actual selling price of the stock when Put will be less than the Put price. If you hold "a Put," viz , the right to deliver Jones 100 shares of stock for which he agrees to pay you $4,500 and you can buy that stock in the market for $2,500, it is very clear you make the difference between $2,500 and $4,500. Therefore, when Puts are bought, a decline in the market is expected, and the profits are made from the decline. The details of a transaction of this kind, such as furnishing the money to buy the stock, and making the delivery to the signer of the contract, is always carried out by your broker. The last few years puts have resulted very profitably. Every time the market has advanced it has been follow d by a greater decline.

Lake Shore on May 8th, 1875, was selling at 72. We find by referring to our books that one of our customers bought a Put on 100 shares of this stock at 70, for thirty days, for which he paid $106.25.

The following is a copy of the Contract :

Negotiated by
TUMBRIDGE & CO.,
Bankers and Brokers in Stock Privileges.
Stocks Bought and Sold on Margins.
2 WALL ST.
P. O. Box 2282.

New York, May 8th, 1875.

For Value Received, – *The Bearer may* DELIVER ME *One Hundred Shares of the Stock of the Lake Shore and Michigan Southern Railroad Company, at Seventy per cent., any time in thirty days from date.*

The undersigned is entitled to ALL DIVIDENDS OR EXTRA DIVIDENDS *declared during the time.*

Expires June 7th, 1875.

1:45 *P. M.*   *Signed* ....

The stock declined during May, to 57⅜ but the contract was not closed until the day of its expiration, when the stock was selling for 61, at which price we bought 100 shares and delivered

A PUT THAT PAID A PROFIT OF $781.75, ON AN INVESTMENT OF $106.25.

BLOWING BUBBLES OF FINANCIAL FROTH.

MASTER JAY GOULD (to Miss Commodore.)—"*Say, Sissy, if I blow and blow, and you blow and blow, which of our bubbles'll go out first? they're nearly the same size now.*"
MISS COMMODORE.—"*Yours, Bubby   You see, I have blown them ever so long, and the bubbles know me.   This one'll last as long as I live, I'm used to water and—after me the deluge.*"
Daily Graphic.

New York Central was once one of the most speculative stocks on the list.   It has made many a man's fortune.   It has been known to advance twenty per cent. in one day. It was the first stock to recover the effects of the panic, and many a one hundred dollar call on it has paid **FIFTEEN HUNDRED DOLLARS.**

Union Pacific for the past two years has been the leader of the market, and has, probably, paid larger profits to holders of privileges than any other stock.   During March, as high as

$2,500 PROFIT WAS MADE ON 100 SHARE CALLS.

So the bubbles may grow or burst, it matters not to the holders of **Privileges.**

Jay Gould has the faculty of turning good or evil to his own advantage. The above represents him with a Grasshopper's assistance throwing stocks overboard, and creating a panic which will enable him to buy back at handsome profits. In May and June when the Grasshopper scare was at its height, the market was very excited and the fluctuations wide.

The following are a few of the privileges negotiated and settled by us for customers during May, 1875:

COST.			PROFIT.
$106.25	Contracts on **Lake Shore** were settled at a profit of	$1,175.00	
106.25	Contracts on **Erie** were settled at a profit of	1,087.50	
106.25	Contracts on **Pacific Mail** were settled at a profit of	900.00	
106.25	Contracts on **Western Union** were settled at a profit of	750.00	

THE SELLING OF OPTION CONTRACTS

Selling Call Options Against a Portfolio

I remember lecturing in Chicago some years ago, and after this talk, during a question-and-answer period, one of my audience said, "I have bought options, but I never knew I could sell them." Well, for every trade—whether in options or clothing or real estate—there must be both a buyer and a seller. It is usually very interesting to my audiences to learn where options come from, who makes them, and why. I'll try to explain the selling of options, the advantages to the seller, the disadvantages, and the pitfalls, for I said at the outset that I would show the good side and the bad.

Options are sold by individuals, funds, trusts and insurance companies, and—as I like to say—by anyone who has what I call "a continuous portfolio of common stocks." One who sells options must be percentage-minded—the man who buys a stock at 50 and expects to get 150 for it is not a prospective seller of options, but the man who is satisfied to take a premium of, say, $300 and for that give a Call on his stock for 90 days, and then repeat that procedure over and over again, is percentage-minded and could do well. *It is my contention that the selling of options against a portfolio is no more speculative than is the owning of such common stocks.*

Consider, if you will, a man (or an institution) who owns 1,000 shares of a stock selling at 50. He sells a Call, good for 90 days, at 50, for which he receives $300 per 100 share Call. This $300 he receives as soon as he sells the option. Let's see what happens if the stock goes up, and also what happens if the stock goes down.

If the stock goes down and is below the Call price when the option expires, the Call will not be exercised. The seller of the Call will still have his stock and will have profited by the $300 which he received for the Option. If he can sell such an option four times a year (and there are four 90-day periods in a year), he will make $1,200 in premiums, or almost 25 per cent per annum on the $5,000 investment.

Let's look at the other side: the stock advances and the stock is selling above the Call price when, or before, the option expires. The stock is "Called" and the seller of the option must deliver stock at 50, less any dividends. He then has:

Sold 100 shares at 50	$5,000
Received $300 for Call	300
Total Received	$5,300

I am sure that after Mr. Trader has had his stock Called and has $5,300 to re-invest, he can think of another stock which he would be willing to buy. Let's say that this stock is also selling around 50, and he buys 100 shares and then sells a Call against it. The stock will either go up or down. If it goes up, he has his $300 premium again for the second Call and he loses his stock. If it goes down, the Call won't be exercised. He has the $300 premium and is at liberty to sell a Call again on the same stock if he cares to do so.

It is just as simple as that and quite automatic. One shouldn't sell a Call at one time and for *one expiration date* on all of his stock, but should try to sell a Call on part today, at today's price, and a Call on part of his holdings at a later date at the current market price in an attempt to have staggered prices and options expiring on different dates, like this:

Sold call 200 at 50, expiring June 20 Premium $600
Sold call 200 at 52 expiring July 7 Premium 600
Sold call 300 at 54 expiring July 18 Premium 900

I believe that there are two pitfalls to avoid in the selling of options: (1) Never sell a Call option unless you own the stock, and (2) Never sell a Put option without the wherewithal to pay for the stock in case it is Put to you. Otherwise, the risk in selling options is no greater, in my opinion —arrived at through years of experience—than the risk in owning like common stocks. For instance, if one had sold Calls freely in the beginning of 1958 *without* owning the stocks, he could have been Called for stock at 50 when it was selling at 80. If one had sold Puts in the summer of 1957 without having sufficient cash to pay for the stock when it was Put to him, he might have had stock Put to him at 50 when it was selling at 30. The return to be had by selling options almost on an investment basis is interesting enough without looking for additional income and additional grief by trying to gain additional premiums.

Before going into the selling of Put options, Straddles, Spreads, Strips and Straps—a word about margins. The New York Stock Exchange has set *minimum* initial margin requirements for the sale of options by customers of its member firms. However, these member firms may increase these requirements according to house policy. The minimum initial margin for the selling of a Put option is 25 per cent of the Put option price, unless the account is "short" the stock which is already adequately margined. The minimum initial margin requirement for the sale of a Call option is 30 per cent of the stock on which the Call is written, unless the Call is written on stock already "long," in which case the "long" stock is already adequately margined. The *minimum* initial margin requirement for the sale of a combination Put and Call (Spread or Straddle) where there is no stock position, is the larger of the two requirements for the separate Put or Call, or 30 per cent.

It must be emphasized that these are *minimum* initial requirements and that they may be increased by the member firm where the customer has his account but they cannot be below these initial requirements as fixed by the rules of the New York Stock Exchange. Before attempting to sell options, arrangements should be made with your stock-exchange broker for the guarantee of such contracts. Your stock-exchange broker will also advise you what the margin requirements are.

When an option is exercised, however, thereby creating a stock position, the position must be fully margined according to stock-exchange requirements.

The Sale of Put Options

An individual (or a company) has $100,000 which he would invest in common stocks. He could buy these stocks in the market or he could sell Put options in an attempt to acquire the stocks a few points below the current market price or to earn premiums from the sale of Put options against the money that he is willing to invest.

For an example: With a stock selling at 50, a man (or a company) sells a Put option at 50 for 90 days, receiving a premium of $300 for each 100-share Put contract. For the $300-premium which he receives at the time that he "makes" the Put contract, he agrees to buy 100 shares at 50 before expiration of the option *if the holder of the option cares to deliver it to him.* The maker of the Put has no choice—he must receive and pay for the stock if it is Put to him. The option is with the holder of the contract. If, before or at the expiration of the option the holder of the contract cares to deliver the stock, the maker of the option must buy 100 shares at 50, which price is reduced by the $300 he received for the option, making the cost to him 47. If the stock is above the Put price, the holder of the Put option will not deliver stock and the writer or maker of the option has benefited by the $300 received for the contract. Here, too, it must be remembered that if it is possible to sell four such Put options in a year (there are four 90-day periods in a year), the annual return will be $1,200 on a possible investment of $5,000.

The operation can be worked on a number of shares of stock or stocks up to the point where the total amount to be paid for the stocks (if the holders of the Puts exercise them), less the premiums received, equals the amount of cash held for investment. To illustrate:

Suppose that Mr. A. and Mr. B. would each like to acquire 1,000 shares of different stocks selling at 50. Mr. A. buys 1,000 shares:

```
100  A  at  50.................... $5,000
100  B  at  50....................  5,000
100  C  at  50....................  5,000
100  D  at  50....................  5,000
100  E  at  50....................  5,000
100  F  at  50....................  5,000
100  G  at  50....................  5,000
100  H  at  50....................  5,000
100  I   at  50....................  5,000
100  J  at  50....................  5,000
```
                    Total Cost.......$50,000

Mr. B. sells a Put option on each stock at 50 for 90 days for $300 premium for each 100-share Put. He has received $3,000. At the expiration of the options, no Puts are exercised, and he has earned $3,000 on his possible investment of $50,000 of cash he is holding for investment, at an annual rate of about 24 per cent.

If the Put options are exercised, he will have an account such as this:

```
Bought 100 A on a/c of Put ............. $5,000
Bought 100 B on a/c of Put .............  5,000
Bought 100 C on a/c of Put .............  5,000
Bought 100 D on a/c of Put .............  5,000
Bought 100 E on a/c of Put .............  5,000
Bought 100 F on a/c of Put .............  5,000
Bought 100 G on a/c of Put .............  5,000
Bought 100 H on a/c of Put .............  5,000
Bought 100 I  on a/c of Put .............  5,000
Bought 100 J  on a/c of Put .............  5,000
```
            Total Cost $50,000

        Less Premiums Received...... 3,000

        Net Cost $47,000

Mr. A's list cost him $50,000, while Mr. B. has acquired the same stocks at a cost of $47,000. It isn't likely that the situation would work out this all-or-none way; probably some Puts would be exercised, some not. But the principle is clear.

So much for selling a Put or Call option. A man sells a Put option if he is willing to have the stock delivered to him. He may be short the stock and willing to cover, or he may have no position in the stock but have funds to pay for the stock and be willing, for a premium, to acquire the stock at a price which may be above the market price for it at the time the Put option is exercised by the holder.

Conversely, if a man owns stock which he would be willing to sell, he sells Call options, and the premium which he receives enhances the selling price if the Call is exercised; if it is not exercised, the premium adds to the income on the stock which he holds.

Buy 100 Shares and Sell Straddle or Buy 200 Shares

Consider the difference, if you will, between these two methods: Mr. A. is bullish on XYZ and buys 200 shares at the market, which is 70. Mr. B. is also bullish and buys 100 shares at 70, and at the same time sells a Straddle at 70 for 90 days for $700. At or before the time the option expires, one of three things will happen:

(1) At the expiration of the contract (neither side having been exercised prior to that date), the market price for the stock is just about the Straddle price. This rarely happens, but it can and sometimes does.

Neither the Put nor the Call is exercised and Mr. B. has gained the $700 premium.

(2) The stock is selling below 70, the Put price, and Mr. B. will have 100 shares delivered to him on the Put option, which will make his position as follows:

Bought 100 shares in market at 70	$7,000
Had 100 shares Put at 70	7,000
Net Cost	$14,000
Less premium received	700
Net Cost of 200 Shares	$13,300

or 66½ for each 100 shares

(3) The stock is above the Call price (70) and Mr. B. will have his 100 shares called from him at 70. His account will look like this:

Sold 100 shares (through Call) at 70	$7,000
Sold Straddle 100 shares—premium	700
	$7,700
Bought 100 shares in market at 70	$7,000
Profit	$ 700

The first situation needs no discussion as it rarely happens. If it does, however, Mr. B. is at liberty to sell another Straddle, having profited by the premium of $700 on an actual investment of $7,000 and a possible investment of $7,000 on the outstanding Put option—or at the rate of 20 per cent per annum.

In the second situation the market is down, but Mr. B. has his 200 shares at a cost of $13,300, whereas Mr. A. has his 200 shares at a cost of $14,000.

In the third situation, we know that Mr. B. made $700.

What Mr. A. made is problematical; it depends on what he did with his stock. If he sold his stock in the market below 73½, he did not do as well as Mr. B.; if he sold it above 73½, he did better than Mr. B. Mr. B.'s method of operation is quite mechanical—each 100 shares of stock he holds is a unit on which he tries to earn as many premiums a year as he can. Each $7,000 he had available for investment is also considered a unit which can earn him a premium, and on this, too, he tries to earn as many premiums as he can each year. Mr. B.'s only problem is to stay in and sell options on stocks which he would be willing to have in his investment portfolio if the Puts are exercised.

Selling Straddles Against a Portfolio

The owner of 100 shares of a stock may be willing either to buy more shares of the stock or to sell out at a premium. In such a situation he can sell a Straddle. A Straddle, as previously defined, is a combination of a Put and a Call, both at the market price of the stock. Let us say that a man sold a Straddle on XYZ at 50 for 90 days, and for it received $500 per 100-share Straddle. By selling the Straddle, he has contracted: (1) to sell 100 shares at 50 any time within 90 days when Called by the holder of the Straddle; (2) to buy 100 shares at 50 any time within 90 days if the holder of the Straddle Puts stock to him. If the Call is exercised, he will have sold his stock at 50 plus the $500 that he received for the option. If the Put is exercised, he will have bought stock at 50, which price is reduced to 45 by the $500 premium. But, you may ask, cannot *both* the Put and the Call be exercised—first the Call before expiration and then, after the Call has been exercised and still before expiration, the Put? Yes, that can happen. A Straddle consists of a Put and a Call—both separate contracts—and the exercise of one does not void the remaining contract. What would be the result to the writer of the Straddle if both contracts were exercised? Well, in the example cited, the trader started with 100 shares. That stock was called, leaving him with no stock, but subsequently he had 100 shares Put to him, so after he sold 100, he then bought 100, and this brought him back to his original position of 100 shares. Finally, he was ahead by the $500 premium which he received.

Selling a Spread Option

While a Spread is an option that isn't bought or sold too much, an explanation of it nevertheless belongs here so that the reader becomes familiar with all kinds of options.

Suppose that instead of selling a Straddle (both the Put and the Call at 50 for 90 days for $500), Mr. Trader sold a Put at 49 and a Call at 51—that's called a 2-point Spread—and instead of receiving $500, as he would for the Straddle, he receives $400 for the Spread. As a rule, the premium received by the seller of the option or paid by the buyer is reduced by $50 for each point Spread. Thus the Spread of 2 points reduces the premium by one point, or $100. This Spread option, like all other options, is traded by negotiation and is sometimes more difficult to make because the "maker" of the option would prefer to have more "cash in hand" and, therefore, would prefer to sell the Straddle. The only advantage in selling a Spread is this: if, at the expiration of the Spread, the stock which was selling at 50 at the making of the Spread is now selling between 49 and 51, chances are that neither the Put nor Call will be exercised; whereas if a Straddle at 50 has been sold, the chances are greater that at least one side of the Straddle, if not both, will be exercised.

Sale of a Strip

A quite recent addition to the family of Stock Options is a contract called a Strip. It is simply a Straddle with an extra Put—in other words, a Put on 200 shares and a Call on 100. The seller of a strip at 50 would contract to buy 200 shares at 50 and/or sell 100 shares at 50. If the sale of a Straddle at 50 would bring the seller $500, then the sale of a Strip would bring about $700. Suppose that a man who had 100 shares of stock selling at 50 were willing to sell a Straddle for $500; that means that he would be willing to sell his stock at 50 plus the $500 premium and/or would be willing to buy 100 shares of additional stock at 50, which would be reduced in cost by the premium of $500 which he received.

In the sale of a Strip on the same stock, if the stock were Called, he would have sold his stock at 50 plus the $700 premium, or at a price equivalent to 57.

On the other hand, if the stock declined and the Puts were exercised, he would have to buy 200 additional shares at 50, which price would be reduced to $46\frac{1}{2}$ on each 100 by reason of the $700 premium received. Therefore, the question must be asked by the seller of a Strip, "Would I

107

be willing to lose my stock at 57 and/or would I be willing to buy 200 additional shares at 46½?" The increased premium for a Strip gives a higher selling price in case the Call is exercised. If the two Puts are exercised, the $700 premium received reduces the cost of the stock by 3½ points for each 100-share Put. Whether a Straddle or a Strip should be sold (assuming that it is possible to sell a Strip) depends on the "market feel" of the seller of the contract.

Selling a Strap

The reverse of the Strip and, also, a cousin of the Straddle is the Strap. It is a form of option contract that was unknown a dozen years ago. It is merely a combination of a Put on 100 shares and Call on 200 shares. To make a comparison: if a Straddle—one Put and one Call—will bring a premium of $500, and a Strip will bring a premium of $700, a Strap will bring a premium of about $800. If the Calls are exercised, the seller of the Strap will have to sell 200 shares at 50, which price will be increased by the $800 premium to an average sale price of 54. However, if the market declines and the one Put is exercised, the maker of the Strap will have to "take" or buy 100 shares at 50, but this price will be reduced to 42 also by reason of the $800 premium which he received for the sale of the Strap.

Selling Call Options Against Convertible Bonds, Warrants, or Preferred Convertible Stocks

There are those who might be called semi-professional or professional traders who own or buy convertible bonds.

These bonds are convertible into common stock of the same company and against these bonds the traders sell Call options on the common stock. Below we see an example of how this is done against "converts." The same method can at times be used against warrants and convertible preferred stocks.

General Telephone convertible 4½'s of 1977 sell at approximately 140, or $1,400 for a $1,000 bond at this writing. The stock at the same time sells at 64⅜. Each $1,000 bond is convertible into 21.74 shares of the common stock. Therefore, five bonds costing $7,000 give the holder the right to convert into 108.7 shares of common stock.

Suppose that the holder of such bonds sells a Call on 100 shares at 64⅜—the market price—for 90 days for $500. One of two results is possible: The Call will not be exercised and the holder of the bonds—the seller of the Call—will benefit by the $500 received for the Call (which will mathematically reduce the cost of the bonds by $500, or 10 points per bond). Or the Call will be exercised, at which time the holder of the bonds will convert into 108.7 shares of stock. He will deliver the 100 shares at the Call price, less dividends, and either hold or sell the odd 8.7 shares. His account will read:

Bought 5 bonds at 140 Cost		$7,000.00
Sold 100 shares stock at 64⅜	$6,437.50	
Received for Call 100 shares	500.00	
Value of remaining shares (8.7) (minimum value)	560.00	
Because if the stock is Called the stock will be above the Call price	$7,497.50	
Profit	$ 497.50	

A study of convertible features of securities might disclose other such opportunities.

The Sale of 6-Month-10-Day-Options

The tax law says, in effect, that the premiums received from the sale of an option must be held in abeyance until the expiration or the exercise of the option. If the contract expires, the premium is ordinary income to the seller of the option. If the option is exercised and it is a Call, the premium is an addition to the proceeds of the sale and, hence, increases the gain, or decreases the loss, on the sale. If the option is exercised and it is a Put, the premium decreases the cost of the stock and, hence, will increase the gain or decrease the loss on the ultimate sale of the stock. The gain or loss on the sale of the stock may be either long term, or short term, depending on the length of time the stock has been held. If a 90-day Call option is sold on a stock after the stock has been held 30 days and the Call is exercised, the time of holding the stock would amount, in all, to approximately 4 months and the gain, if any (including the premium received for the sale of the Call), would be taxed as *short*-term gain. If the stock in question had been held for over three months when the Call was sold and the Call was exercised at expiration, then the stock in question would have been held for more than 6 months, and any profit, plus the premium received from the sale of the Call, would have been *long*-term gain. For that reason options are sold for 6 months and 10 days, or longer. It may be that the prospective seller of options does not own the stock for which a Call is bid, but is willing to buy such stock and then sell the Call which is wanted. If a stock is selling at 50 and a 6-month-and-10-day Call contract is bid for, the prospective seller of the Call may buy stock in the market so as to sell the Call. Of course, if the Call is not exercised, the premium received is ordinary income.

But let us explore the tax possibilities if the Call is exercised. Let us assume that a man has bought stock at 50 and has sold a 6-month-and-10-day Call for, let us say, $500. The stock, held for more than 6 months, has gone up to 70 and is Called. The seller has a $500 long-term profit. However, the alert trader may be able to get a sizeable tax benefit. *Before* the Call is exercised but when the stock has been held for more than 6 months, he may sell his stock in the market and take a long-term profit of $2,000. But he still owes stock at 50 on account of the Call which he sold. After having sold his stock at 70 to take a long-term gain, he immediately repurchases stock at 70, and *this* stock he delivers on his Call a few days later, when the Call is exercised. He now has a $2,000 long-term gain and a short-term loss of $2,000, less the premium of $500 which he received for the Call—a $2,000 long-term gain and a $1,500 short-term loss.

While short-term losses may no longer offset long-term gains at the ratio of $1 of short-term capital loss against $2 of long-term gain (as was the law some years ago), there are many situations in which having a long-term gain and a short-term loss is tax-wise.

Just as a buyer of an option can capitalize, tax-wise, on

111

a long-term option which he bought, so the seller of an option can benefit through proper treatment of options which he has sold. Of course, there is no guarantee that the holder of a long-term Call option will wait till the expiration of his 6 months "plus" before exercising his contract. It may be that a stock could go from 50 to 75 or 80 in half the life of the option, and the holder of the contract, not wanting to lose his profit, may exercise his contract. In such a case the holder of the stock on which the Call was sold may want to buy an additional 100 shares of stock to deliver against the Call and thus maintain his long position in the original stock until it becomes long-term gain.

A summary of the income tax treatment of premiums paid for by the buyer of options and those received by the seller of options has been added as an appendix. This review of tax treatment has been prepared by a leading New York tax-expert and is based on the 1954 tax law as amended and now current.

In conclusion, may I reiterate that I do not contend that all those interested in securities must trade in Put and Call options. I do feel, however, that this part of Wall Street procedure should be understood by all those who trade in securities, since a time may well come when such understanding can be put to good use in their securities transactions. It is my hope that this book has shed light on the option business, for those who are interested in securities and knew nothing about options, and also for those who had just a little knowledge of the business and wanted to know more about it.

APPENDIX

INCOME TAX TREATMENT OF "PUT" AND "CALL" OPTION TRANSACTIONS

Under the Internal Revenue Code of 1954

Revenue Ruling 58-234

and Other Rulings in Effect May 19, 1958

Prepared by

Brach, Gosswein & Lane
Certified Public Accountants

Description of Transaction

I. PUTS

    A. As to the purchaser (optionee) of put

        1. Tax treatment of amount paid for put (premium) prior to its being exercised or its expiration

        2. Tax treatment of amount paid for put (premium) when put is not exercised but is held to expiration

        3. Tax treatment of amount paid for put (premium) when put is exercised

        4. Acquisition of a put as a short sale

Income Tax Treatment

Amount paid is to "be carried to a deferred account as a capital expenditure made in an incompleted transaction entered into for profit."

Amount paid is capital loss for the year in which the put expired by limitation of time. If put has been held for not more than 6 months loss is short-term. If it has been held for more than 6 months loss is long-term. (Specific provision in Section 1234 I.R.C. 1954.) But if transaction falls within exception in (5) the amount paid is an addition to the cost of the related stock.

Upon exercise of put the purchaser (optionee) sells the property to which the put relates to the writer (optionor) for the option price. The amount paid for the put is a reduction of the proceeds of sale.

The acquisition of a put constitutes a short sale. If, at the time the short sale is made, taxpayer holds the related security which he has held for not more than 6 months, or, if while the short sale is open he acquires such security, the holding period of the security does not start until the date of the closing of the short sale. The exercise of the option, or the expiration thereof is considered as the closing of the short sale. (Sec. 1233(b) I.R.C. 1954) (This point is not covered in Revenue Ruling 58-234.) But see exception in (5) following.

Description of Transaction

I. PUTS *(Continued)*

   A. As to the purchaser (optionee) of put *(continued)*

      5. Exception if put is acquired on same date as related security is purchased

      6. Tax treatment if put is sold

   B. As to writer (issuer or optionor) of put

      1. Tax treatment of amount received for writing or issuing put (premium) prior to its being exercised or its expiration

Income Tax Treatment

If put is acquired on the same day on which the security identified as intended to be used in exercising the put is acquired, and if the put, if exercised, is exercised through the sale of the property so identified, the acquisition of the put is not treated as a short sale. However, if the put is not exercised, the cost of the put must be added to the cost of the related stock (Section 1233(c) I.R.C. 1954). An informal and unpublished ruling holds that, if taxpayer sells the put instead of exercising it, the exception of Section 1233(c) will not be applicable and the acquisition of the put will be considered a short sale.

Gain or loss on sale is capital gain or loss (except in the case of a dealer); long-term, if put has been held for more than 6 months, short-term, if held for not more than 6 months. (Section 1234 I.R.C. 1954.) If Section 1233(b) is applicable, by reason of long position in related security, gain on sale of put will be short-term, even though put has been held for more than 6 months if sale of put is considered "closing" of short sale. No opinion is expressed on this point for reason that law and regulations are not clear.

Amount received is to be carried in a deferred account. No tax consequences until put is exercised or expires.

Description of Transaction

I. PUTS (*Continued*)

    B. As to writer (issuer or optionor) of put (*continued*)

        2. Tax treatment of amount received for writing or issuing put (premium) when put is not exercised but expires

        3. Tax treatment of amount received for writing or issuing put (premium) when put is exercised by purchaser thereof

            (a) Holding period of security purchased by exercise of put by purchaser thereof

II. CALLS

    A. As to purchaser (optionee) of call

        1. Tax treatment of amount paid for call (premium) prior to its being exercised or its expiration

        2. Tax treatment of amount paid for call (premium) when call is not exercised but is held to expiration

Income Tax Treatment

Amount received constitutes ordinary income for the year in which the failure of the holder to exercise the option becomes final. This is so, because, under Section 61, I.R.C. 1954, all income is ordinary income unless otherwise provided, and Section 1234, which deals with options to buy and sell, contains no reference to the *gain* from the failure to exercise an option.

Upon exercise of put, the writer (optionor) buys the security at the option price. The amount received for writing the option (premium) constitutes an offset against the amount paid in determining the net cost basis of the security purchased.

Holding period of the security purchased starts the date the put is exercised, and not the date the put was issued.

Amount paid is to "be carried to a deferred account as a capital expenditure made in an incompleted transaction entered into for profit."

Amount paid is capital loss for the year in which the call expired by limitation of time. If call has been held for not more than 6 months, loss is short-term. If it has been held for more than 6 months, loss is long-term (specific provision in Section 1234 I.R.C. 1954).

Description of Transaction

II. CALLS *(Continued)*

A. As to purchaser (optional) of call *(continued)*

3. Tax treatment of amount paid for call (premium) when call is exercised

   (a) Holding period of security acquired through exercise of call

4. Acquisition of call as short sale

5. Call as substantially identical property

6. Tax treatment if call is sold

B. As to writer (issuer or optionor) of call

1. Treatment of amount received for writing or issuing call (premium) prior to its being exercised or its expiration

Income Tax Treatment

Amount paid is an addition to the cost of the stock purchased on the exercise of the call.

Holding period of the security purchased starts on the date the call is exercised and not the date the call was acquired.

The acquisition of a call (unlike the acquisition of a put) does not constitute a short sale. Section 1233(b) does not relate to calls.

The call and the related security are not substantially identical properties. Hence, gain on sale of call held for more than 6 months is long-term gain, even though a short sale of the related security was made during period call was held. (Letter ruling dated February 27, 1957, published in Tax Services)

Gain or loss on sale is capital gain or loss (except in the case of a dealer); long-term if call has been held for more than 6 months, short-term if held for not more than 6 months. Short sale of related security does not kill holding period (see [5] above). (Section 1234, I.R.C. 1954)

Amount received is to be carried in a deferred account. No tax consequences until call is exercised or expires.

Description of Transaction

II. CALLS (*Continued*)

  B. As to writer (issuer or optionor) of call (*continued*)

    2. Tax treatment of amount received for writing or issuing call (premium) when call is not exercised but expires

    3. Tax treatment of amount received for writing or issuing call (premium) when call is exercised

Income Tax Treatment

Amount received constitutes ordinary income for the year in which the failure the holder to exercise the option becomes final. This is so, because, under Section 61, I.R.C. 1954 all income is ordinary income unless otherwise provided and Section 1234, which deals with options to buy and sell, contains no reference to the *gain* from the failure to exercise an option.

Upon exercise of call, the writer (optionor) sells the security at the option price. The amount received for writing the option (premium) is added to the amount received as the option price, in arriving at the gain or loss on the sale of the security. (IT 3835 C.B. 1947-1, p. 53)

Description of Transaction

III. GENERAL PROVISIONS

Adjustments for cash dividends, stock rights, stock dividends and stock splits

Income Tax Treatment

Under common trade practice, the purchaser (optionee) of a call who exercises it is entitled to receive from the writer (optionor) an *amount equal to* all cash dividends, regular or extra, plus the market value of all rights accrued on the security involved (determined on the basis of the first sale of rights on the day the stock sells ex-rights). To reflect this right, the option price is reduced by such amount and the purchaser (optionee) pays the writer (optionor) the adjusted option price. A similar adjustment of the option price is made in the case of a put. In that case, the price which the writer (optionor) pays the purchaser (optionee) is reduced by the amount of such cash dividends and the value of such rights. The number of shares to which the option relates is increased to reflect the additional shares which would be received during the life of the option on the shares originally covered by the option by reason of stock dividends or stock splits and the option price per share is correspondingly reduced, the *total* option price remaining unchanged. The cash adjustment for cash dividends and rights is not ordinary income but is a reduction of the option price, whether the option price is adjusted or the cash adjustment is made separately. (Revenue Ruling 58-234) (see also IT 4007, C.B. 1950-1, p. 11 and Revenue Rulings 56-153 and 56-211)